PRAISE FOR

INTO THE GRAY

"Knowing Michelle as I do, reading *Into the Gray* felt like a sacred privilege. Her excruciating honesty, her vulnerable confessions, her insights into spiritual abuse and her resilience ... were both riveting and humbling. But what I appreciated most was how she neither tied off the story with saccharine platitudes nor left me hopeless. The metamorphosis remains open. Brutally beautiful."

Brad Jersak, Dean of Theology & Culture,
St. Stephen's University, New Brunswick

"For the past twenty years, I have been counseling people who were deeply damaged by spiritual abuse and toxic religious indoctrination. It would have been useful to give them a copy of Michelle Collins' book, *Into the Gray*. I'm grateful I will be able to give it to others now. *Into the Gray* is a profoundly insightful, courageously honest, refreshingly practical, and deeply heartfelt accounting of what it means to truly be free from the wounds caused by harmful religion."

Jim Palmer, Critically acclaimed author of
Divine Nobodies and *Inner Anarchy*

"Deconstruction is not something one chooses to do, most of us are dragged kicking and screaming into it. It can cost us everything, friends, family, God, even we go through the existential wringer. It's why this book is so important. As unique as Michelle's story is—it is our story too. Hearing that we aren't alone, that we aren't crazy, and that we aren't backsliding makes all the difference as we navigate our deconstruction. With vulnerability and wisdom she bears all on the page in a way that doesn't leave us paralyzed but rather inspired to keep moving forward into the great unknown."

Phil Drysdale, Founder of TheDeconstructionNetwork.com and host of The Phil Drysdale Show

"When I read Michelle's book, I felt pulled along by association. I identified with so much of what she has experienced on her road through deconstruction. I insist everyone's journey is different and unique, but there are also a lot of similarities. If you are questioning your beliefs, feel like you are losing your faith, or if you struggle with your relationship to the church (or maybe all three), this book will help you realize that you are not alone, that what you are experiencing is becoming more prevalent, and that you will be okay! It is disturbing and comforting at the same time. Even though Michelle writes descriptively as she shares with us her fascinating story, you may walk away with plenty of prescriptive advice on how to navigate the waters of deconstruction in a healthier manner."

David Hayward, The NakedPastor

"I read *Into the Gray* in its entirety, and it immediately drew me in like a friend who was having an honest conversation that was raw and everything I needed it to be. There are those who try to tell people how to feel and what to feel, and Michelle does not do that in this structured meandering of her life and understanding, inside and out. She shares her experience and graciously gives the reader room for their experience without judgment. The vivid imagery she includes helps the reader to see and feel with her throughout her expression of deconstruction. I love her deeply personal approach, coupled with the fact that she is not alone claiming to be anything other than a human being wrestling with faith and the collision of what she was told versus what she lived. Michelle pulls in others for this conversation that you will want to hear.

From the psychological Kafka, the lay person, tadpoles and butterflies, and Luke Skywalker, all are voices from whom she gleans wisdom. It left me smiling and nodding in agreement, and at other points, pondering things I had not before considered. This book is an emotional expression of bare and intimate honesty that could make you feel uncomfortable. If you are willing to go there, it could help you confront some of your own thoughts and experiences while even helping you process. It is worth the read and worth pausing at times to process because there is meat on these bones. Weighty enough to engage the intellectual with references galore and yet personable and full of heart. If you want a thought-provoking ride down the coast with the top down, this book will blow wind through your hair and cause you to reflect on issues you may not have considered. It is just that interactive."

PK Langley, Author of *Religious Deconstruction:*
The Frustrated Grace Series

"Michelle Collin's *Into the Gray* is a wise, feisty, and compassionate guide for those who are in the midst of deconstructing and reconstructing their faith, experiencing a disorienting faith shift, or have experienced life-altering religious trauma. Michelle's down-to-earth writing style, provocative depth, vulnerable storytelling, relevant psychological insights, and breadth of knowledge concerning issues of faith makes this a vital resource for your healing journey!"

Mark Karris, Author of *Religious Refugees*

"I've had a lot of physical pain in my life due to different injuries, one of which is a herniated disc in my low back. I played softball with this injury for a year and a half without knowing that it was actually an injury, I kept being told it was just muscle tightness. I had a symptoms that didn't line up with how this injury is typically displayed. It was infuriating to never know the reason for my pain. I finally was diagnosed after I demanded imaging. After all that time, I had the thing I was searching for, validation. I felt relief! Even though I had lived with all this pain and had people telling me it was something else entirely, I had validation for my experiences. It didn't erase my pain, but I felt like it was finally real.

This book made me think of that. I've gone through the process of deconstruction now for almost the same amount of time as Michelle. She is the one who initiated it for me (thanks mom) while she started questioning the 'limits' of grace. This book highlighted everything I felt and then some. It validated my experiences without giving me limitations for what was acceptable. I'm very grateful to have my mother as a resource and a sounding board through my process. I feel like she brings so many concepts to the table for our contemplation without shoving it in our faces. I was fascinated to learn about things like the apperceptive mass, imaginal cells, and the stages of power. So many things that put my experiences in new lights that helped me understand myself more.

What I appreciated most was that while the book shared psychological concepts, it also gave an avenue for them. There is application involved that doesn't leave me feeling like, 'now what?' I felt connected to everything, maybe because of experience, but I think also because of the experience of the writer. There's no pretentious statement of facts. She lays it all out there for us to see alongside the concepts that helped her understand the process. It makes it accessible, not just intellectual."

Amanda Cisi, *extremely* proud daughter

INTO

THE MENTAL AND EMOTIONAL AFTERMATH

THE

OF SPIRITUAL DECONSTRUCTION

GRAY

Michelle Collins

First Edition

Cover design and layout by Rafael Polendo (polendo.net)

Unless otherwise identified, all Scripture quotations in this publication are taken from the New Revised Standard Version of the Bible, copyright © 1989 by the National Council of the Churches of Christ in the U.S.A. Used by permission. All rights reserved.

ISBN 978-1-938480-80-5

This volume is printed on acid free paper and meets ANSI Z39.48 standards.

Printed in the United States of America

Published by Quoir
Oak Glen, California

www.quoir.com

DEDICATION

To those who have fallen into the trenches with me.

TABLE OF CONTENTS

FOREWORD

When Michelle asked me to write the foreword for this book, I immediately said yes, not because she wrote one for my book *Heretic!*, or because she is a part of the growing Quoir family, but because I value her insights and perspectives more than 99.9% of those I've come across in my thirty-eight years of life. And look, that's not meant as a knock against others; I just respect the hell out of Michelle and think that what she has to offer the world is beyond priceless. Truly, I would be remiss to pass up the opportunity to be a part of her first book.

As you dig into the meat of this literary tour de force, I can only think that you'll understand why I lavish Michelle with such praise. Not only is it apparent how gifted a writer she is, but it's also apparent that she has a firm grasp on what spiritual deconstruction is and is not, which, given how so many people are going through it, makes this the timeliest of projects.

First and foremost, what deconstruction is: Deeply personal. As Michelle will discuss at length, there is no formula to be had. There is no "twelve-step process," or anything remotely similar. Sure, some of our processes will mirror that of others', but at the end of the day, each and every one of us who have deconstructed—or, put more accurately, are in the thick of deconstructing—are having a uniquely subjective experience. This book then, while tackling the psychological impact of challenging one's faith—Michelle is, after all, currently working on her psychology doctorate—is primarily from the perspective of a single, subjective spiritual sojourner. And this is a good thing! It means that while you will find psychological and theological meat here, what's probably even more important and pertinent to Michelle's thesis is that those who are reading this will have found a kindred spirit. And as such, perhaps they won't feel so alone as they set out on their individual spiritual journeys.

And that's the crux of the matter: Whenever you notice a crack in your faith, the Universe can suddenly appear like a cold and lonely place. Whereas your church community was once a place of solace and comfort, it too often turns into a place of shame and trauma the minute you start to show doubt or skepticism. Everything takes a one-eighty. Grief then sets in. And it's not pretty. Michelle then, while not claiming to be an expert on anything, is at least an expert on this. But that's the beauty of this book. It's real. It's raw. It's revealing. And it's the perfect antidote to those books that claim to be an authority on this matter.

So, as you read *Into the Gray*, keep all of this in mind. Assuming that you are either deconstructing or know someone who is, keep in mind that your story will look a little bit different. Your psychology is a little bit different. Your fears … a little bit different. Your anxieties, your hopes, your pain, your brushes with bliss, your trauma, your moments of joy … all a little bit different. That's the scary part about all of this, but it is also the beautiful part. As Fr. Richard Rohr might say, everything belongs. That means you belong. That means I belong. That means Michelle belongs. And as painful as it sounds, that means our personal deconstruction stories belong. Again, please keep this in mind.

Have an open mind and an inviting heart. Listen to Michelle's story. See where it resonates with you. Notice where it differs. But do all of this with the comforting knowledge that we have among us a strong, powerful woman who is willing to vulnerably articulate her struggles and how she has overcome them, not through some fabricated or formulaic process, but by learning how to accept that it's okay to doubt, that it's okay to not have all the answers, and that it's okay to live in the gray.

— MATTHEW J. DISTEFANO
AUTHOR, PODCASTER, SOCIAL WORKER,
AND HIP-HOP ARTIST

PREFACE

So here it is! My musings, stories, and sometimes my tirades, regarding my journey through what has come to be known as deconstruction. I felt that a preface would be helpful to explain my emotional state during the time I was writing. While I thought I would be able to put all of this down in a relatively short amount of time, I was wrong. Why? Because this particular journey takes time. It takes experience. It takes pain.

Somewhere along the way, I realized I needed a break. The emotions were overwhelming, and I began to doubt that I could explain it well enough. The subject is important, and I was sure I would not do justice to the experience or what others have gone through. I also realized that I had some personal work to do that was directly affected by this process.

Somewhere about six or seven months into the writing process, I hit a wall. I just could not write anymore. I was struggling with so much anger and much of it was self-directed. I decided that it was time to confront myself before I could continue through this maze of emotions and beliefs. I started therapy with a wonderful, friendly therapist and I quickly found that, while she did nothing wrong, there was not enough structure for me. I need structure!

Additionally, she was much more focused on what I was writing about for herself than my personal work at the time. I do not hold her responsible for that, it only served as an example of how widespread and difficult this discussion is. She repeatedly told me of a list of people to whom she could direct me; those in need of something with regard to this conversation. And here I thought we were few and far between. It was at that point that someone introduced me to personal life coaching.

I bid adieu to my therapist and started working on a weekly basis with a life coach who quite honestly pissed me off … a lot. He also made me cry … a lot. I hate that anyone had to see those emotions. Somewhere along the way, I found what he was saying had a positive effect. While initially I had been half-assing it, I found myself suddenly seeing results. I had to get very honest with myself about myself. I had to ask questions about my past beliefs and why I was so easily swayed without even investigating my beliefs. I had to confront personal relationships that had direct effects on who I am today. All that to say, it took work on me before I could work on this, but they were related.

Much of what I wrote has been done so over a period of over a year. I am certain that you will see many times where my voice changes, my understanding changes, because that is what happens when you share from your heart over a period time. You change! You begin to see things differently.

So, this is your warning, I can be sad, I can be angry, and I can be philosophical, but I am always me, just varying voices of me.

I have included some stories that pushed me into this deconstructive process. They were very difficult; however, they failed to reach the level of actual religious abuse that many have experienced in this process. They may sound as though I am complaining, but I am leaving them in as they were the main reasons I walked (or was shoved) away from my religious tradition and into this place of darkness and questions. I have also included small blurbs of other people's experiences as they were shared with me in multiple text messages, emails, and private messages. I have agreed to keep those identities private but felt they added to the point I am trying to make.

One thing that I truly wanted to "warn" you about as you read through my thoughts and experiences is that I am a very sarcastic person, and it only gets worse when I am angry. Please know that in my amateurish attempts at humor, I am not making fun of this process nor do I think it is a funny situation. Sarcasm is my defense mechanism; it is how I deal with those areas in which I struggle the most. You will definitely notice it. I also found myself taking many "sidebars" throughout the writing process. These are generally sarcastic comments regarding the subject matter and how it pertained to my beliefs from long ago.

Okay, enough of me trying to explain away my foibles and insecure rantings. Here we go …

INTRODUCTION

It started as a whisper … a small soft question in the dark recesses of my mind. It was a random thought that passed quickly and caused only a momentary pause in my day. After all, it was nothing more than a verse that I had heard and quoted many times over the years. It all seems so dramatic now, but it did not start that way. I had not pondered the term deconstruction until just recently. As a matter of fact, had someone asked me about the term as it pertains to a belief system, I would not have had an answer. It simply never crossed my mind. I am embarrassed to say that my belief system had been handed down traditionally from my childhood, and as it was often foreign to others around me, I already felt that we were far advanced from historic Christian ideology. I mean after all; we spoke in tongues and raised our hands in worship. Of course, we were on the cutting edge. To question what I believed would have indicated a lack of faith to those I knew in church, never mind pulling apart the belief and finding its foundation.

The whisper returned often and grew progressively louder. It became something I could not ignore. The only choice was to examine the whisper and find out what was on the other side.

"For our sake he made him to be sin who knew no sin, so
that in him we might become the righteousness of God."

2 COR. 5:21

At first, I could not understand why this thought refused to leave
me alone. After a bit I realized that I had spent most of my life trying not to lose that which I had never done anything to attain. That
was revelatory to me! I had spent most of my time trying to be good
enough only to realize repeatedly that I could not be and then feeling
bereft. I asked others their understanding of this verse and, in most
cases, was told the same things I had always thought. My pastor could
not answer my questions and told me to put them on a metaphorical
shelf until such a time as I could understand it. But that was not good
enough. The whisper would not stop!

John Caputo, in *What Would Jesus Deconstruct,* saw the process of
deconstruction in a way that "things are made to tremble by their own
inner impulse, by a force that will give them no rest, that keeps forcing itself to the surface, forcing itself out, making the thing resolve."
My experience with personal deconstruction felt exactly like this …
I did not choose it, and have many times wanted to go back. It just
happened and still continues to happen. It is a painful process that is
exacerbated by loneliness and anger. I have asked myself over and over
how I could have been as stupid as to just accept what I was fed like a
small child that is unable to feed itself.

Many times, I was told to just "be like Christ" as though it were
a simple process to execute or even internalize. That very thought
must be deconstructed as there are so many views of Christ. How
Jesus would conduct himself in any instance is subjective based on
the belief system of the individual. There is an objective truth to how

Jesus would act, and we can find it, but it requires that we step outside of our perspective and understand that we may be in the wrong.

My deconstruction has been in full swing for quite some time. Every time I begin to feel as though I may be finding solid doctrinal ground again, I find that I have only just begun. Every answer produces numerous new questions as the rabbit holes go deeper. Many who have experienced this process will stop along the way, deciding that they have reached the apex of necessary understanding, then closing their eyes and minds once again to anything new. Cognitive dissonance will once again rule the day, and all will be well.

It takes courage to continue this journey, and as I must assess my levels of courage daily, I hold no one guilty that decides they have had enough. For myself, however, I have reached the conclusion that the only way out of the process is through the process.

Please do not assume, however, that I am some expert on the subject matter. Far from it, I am a Sojourner in this process, wandering in the darkness, trying to make sense of what I see and feel. It is daunting at best! As I try to explain my journey, please keep in mind that I do not profess total comprehension, nor do I know how this all ends. I am just trying to start a conversation that I believe is vital for all of us on an emotional and mental level. Working through our feelings on a difficult subject matter will undoubtedly bring up issues and we will spend great amounts of time feeling alone.

That is my one hope with writing all of this down, that you will not feel alone in your journey but will recognize that while my journey is mine and your journey may resemble it in some fashion, the only thing that makes them the same is that we will be affected in some manner. I feel a large sense of responsibility to explain my journey so that it makes sense to others.

As I have not seen anyone approach it from the perspective that I have chosen, I endeavor to speak for a lot of people's experience and that scares the hell out of me because I do not know that I am able, but here goes ...

PERSONAL HISTORY

I remember as a child sitting in Sunday school and enjoying the feeling of learning about God. I have always had the ability to retain most of what I learn, and as such, I always knew all the names of the characters on the felt board. I knew all the stories, all the points, that would be made regarding the lesson. While this foundational knowledge is important, I find in its process the beginnings of a works mentality. When I performed well and answered all the questions, my teachers were impressed and praised me for my understanding. When asked to *not* answer a question but to go in order to give someone else a chance, I felt rebuked and rejected. I had already begun to learn that knowledge and "works" equaled acceptance and being the best in the room was a necessity.

I also remember Bible races. This game involved the children having a closed Bible in front of them. The teacher would then state a reference for a verse, and everyone would immediately jump for their Bible and race to see who could find the verse first. Once found, that child would stand up, recite the verse, and win the round. I was a champion at this game. In my quest for dominance, I stepped on many other fragile egos, but all I understood was the need to win both the game and approval. This, of course, led to praise from my instructors, in turn, leading to further acceptance in my home. Every parent wants their child to succeed, but I was already on a course of needing acclamation to prove worth and seeing all of life, including a relationship with God, as a competition that must be won.

" ... not by works of righteousness which we have done, but according to His mercy He saved us, through the washing of regeneration and renewing of the Holy Spirit, whom He poured out on us abundantly through Jesus Christ our savior, that having been justified by His grace we should become heirs according to the hope of eternal life."

TITUS 3:5-7

While I could find and recite the verses in record time, the meaning of the words did not seem to seep into my heart. I never felt good enough and was always looking for the next chance to impress. My whole life became an act in which I showed only what I thought people wanted to see. I allowed very few people to know me.

It did not help that my home life was dysfunctional, and I struggled to hide all the embarrassment of an abusive household. My grandmother was severely impacted by abuse from her father and stepmother. Told often that she had little worth, she seemed to identify with this idea in that she did not often have kind words or actions for her children. It was termed discipline, but she often was somewhat physically abusive and emotionally distant. Every time I was disciplined by my grandmother, it was with the understanding that she made her points in a physical manner because she "loved me". I firmly believe that my mother suffered in the same manner and was adversely affected by this same attitude of trying to be good enough as well as looking for love.

My grandparents and my mother told me they loved me, but love did not look right, and I firmly believe this is another reason that my relationship with God has suffered through the years. I did not trust love and being told that God was love just made the understanding of the emotion even harder. How could someone who was love, allow so much upheaval and pain? How could a loving God want me when I felt like no one in my life did?

I truly believe that many people can relate to my questions and desire for acceptance. Just daily observing others around me allows for one to see disillusionment, anger, pain, and despondency, and that is just from Christians. As sad as this thought is, there are many broken Christians going through life attempting to be better and to find acceptance through their victories rather than in Christ. Many are working themselves into exhaustion with the hope that their accomplishments will translate into an engraved name on a plaque in the church lobby. This then would be proof they made a difference somewhere to someone. For many, churches are places with a spotlight, a pulpit in which to address their concerns or a stage in which to highlight their talents. Anyone who has ever served in the inner workings of a church can tell you that serving is difficult and, in many cases, is done for the wrong reasons.

Not long ago, I began to feel restless and in need of doing something different. I began to write in my journal every day and explore what God was saying in His word. This was eye opening to me as I heard the word preached all my life but was never quite sure how to apply it to myself. I enjoyed a good amount of time and many journals worth of revelation from God when suddenly … I did not hear anything. That familiar sense of despondency crept back in.

I was positive I had done something incorrect or had some secret sin in my life that was keeping me from hearing God. It was deeply troubling as I still equated my personal spiritual success with what I was doing *for* God rather than who I was *in* God. I went to my husband and explained my problem and we prayed together yet still nothing. I continued in my habit of rising early and reading the Word and journaling. And yet, in the morning, as I sat on my couch trying to encourage myself to keep going, I broke down and cried and like a little girl asked God for the answer to the problem. His answer was life-changing and started me down a path of confusion but also intrigue. He answered simply, *Michelle, you don't know how to be a daughter!*

I immediately agreed but also jumped to my own defense. I said I was never shown. My own father never wanted to be in my life, or so it seemed, and left while I was very young. I had no experience of a relationship like that. I had a vague idea of the "perfect father/daughter relationship" but no outlet in which to experience it. I watched my husband with my daughters and saw that stereotypical "apple of his eye" look when he played with them, but I had never had anyone look at me like that. It was a painful realization, but one I was ready to remedy. I agreed to take this journey with God, but I did know deep inside me that it would be an incredible struggle. And it has been. There are days when I struggle to hold my head up because for the moment, I cannot see myself the way God says he sees me. There are also days in which I catch a glimpse of what it feels like to be a cherished daughter, and it is in those moments that I decide to continue because I know it will be worth it in the end.

One of the first ideas that I felt challenged with was my identity as a daughter of God. My early childhood understanding of God was harsh and angry. I was told repeatedly at a young age that God was always watching. It was ominous and came with an overwhelming fear that I could not be imperfect. The consequences were much more severe than a spanking or time in my room; I mean with God we are talking about eternal consequences. So, I strived for perfection in everything. It is not possible. Even knowing this, I worked hard to measure up to everyone's expectations, taking no time to decide what I liked, who I was, or what I wanted to do. I just performed and tried to stay out of trouble. So, when challenged to be a daughter, it was with this same perfected expectation—perform.

I felt better for a while because in trying to do something with that goal in mind, I felt like there was momentum. I challenged myself to spend more time with God, reading my Bible, praying, going to church, and volunteering for *everything*. In the end, I was exhausted. Interestingly, I know I am not alone. I have heard many express the same thing.

METAMORPHOSIS—PART I

Not too long ago, I was introduced to the subject of metamorphosis. As a child, we all learn about caterpillars becoming butterflies and what a fanciful transition it is. I do not remember a lot of detail surrounding the process when it was discussed, just the outcome, the beautiful, fairy-like butterfly with patterned wings and little feelers on its head. As most little girls, I remember thinking about the ability to fly. How exciting it must be to get a new body along with new ways in which to see the world. It's fanciful; it's somewhat like a fairy tale. It is only as you get older that you encounter the actual process. It is no less fanciful and amazing, yet there is a deeper awareness that occurs at some point.

Recently, I started a class to become a certified life coach. As there are so many life-coaching certifications available, I was unsure where to begin. I tend to lean toward the gold standard when attempting a new venture, so I did some research as to which governing body would be the place to start. Once accomplished, I used their list of life coaching classes to determine which to take. You would be amazed at how many types of coaching there are, and as such, I basically had to choose blindly. I ended up at a "Deep Transformation" coaching class. I did not know what to expect but was excited about a new experience.

I love learning and am consciously endeavoring to learn as much as a I can in many different areas, so this was just another on the path.

Before starting the class, I was provided course materials. It was an initial 10-week class followed by two additional multi-week classes to obtain the actual coaching certification. It is a journey that takes some time. The introduction provided a short podcast in which the details of the overall experience were given as well as an introduction of the instructor and his background.

As I listened to the opening, my eyes were growing wider and wider. I was suddenly aware of tears, and by the end of the short podcast, I could do no more than lay my head on the desk and cry. It was as though someone climbed into my thoughts and emotions and laid out all that I had experienced in the last several years. Up until that point, I refer to this experience as deconstruction and was convinced it had only to do with my religious beliefs and their examination. It had not occurred to me that within that process was the possibility, and probability, of an examination of not only my beliefs, but also my life, and ultimately my being.

Sounds dramatic, right? Anyone who has traveled very far down this road knows, however, that it *is* incredibly dramatic and disrupting and emotional, and … well you get the point!

So, what does this have to do with butterflies? First, I should explain that I have a good amount of weekly homework within this certification, an obligation to be coached by someone in the class, and to coach another person within the class at least 4 times each over the 10 weeks. Much of what you experience and learn comes into the process, and it is a deeply analytical process … at least for me. I tend to get stuck on a point and have a hard time moving forward until I completely dissect that one thing. This is where the butterflies come in.

In one of the first classes, we were provided an hour-long video to watch that included some startling transformations in the animal and insect worlds. Nature is truly amazing and while we may know some of these things anecdotally, it is in the details we find magic. Within this video, the subject of the caterpillar-to-butterfly metamorphosis was broached. I want to walk through this process with you, hoping you will see the correlations to the experience of deconstruction.

WHAT IS DECONSTRUCTION?

" Deconstruction" has become somewhat of a buzzword within the theological world. As many people wrestle with how beliefs play out in the "real" world, there is often the realization that *talking* about a belief can be much easier than *walking* out the belief. It can be disillusioning. It can be devastating. So, what exactly does deconstruction mean?

Recently, during a conversation, I was reminded of how important it is to define terminology and to define as accurately as possible that which I am describing. In no other conversation I can imagine is this more important than that of deconstruction. In a traditional, philosophical sense, "deconstruction" is a term coined by Jacques Derrida. Its core definition or ideal is that of the structural unity of text. Ironically and somewhat humorously, Derrida himself claimed that "deconstruction is necessarily complicated and difficult to explain since it actively criticizes the very language needed to explain it."

So, while Derrida recognized that deconstruction is not an analysis, critique, or method, he also affirms that these terms are best used until they can be replaced. So, with this in mind, my goal in discussing deconstruction is to analyze and critique a belief system and why it is so emotionally charged in its process. Basically, it means the critical analysis of a philosophical position and the assumptions that accompany the position.

For my intentions here, I would say that I am seeking to understand the psychological and emotional implications of questioning a long-held belief or figuring out why we think a certain way. What is the genesis of your position on any given subject? Does it progress from a question all the way to a studied history of the subject, or does it simply come from a familial or religious tradition? While this could be true of any kind of belief such as political or educational, my focus is that of a closely held religious belief. For some reason, a religious belief seems to be emotionally charged to the point of defining us as a person. For many, their beliefs on any given subject come from their upbringing and their parent's thoughts on the subject. Is that wrong? Right or wrong would depend upon where your parents received their information. See how difficult it can get?

So, do people just decide one day that they are going to change the way they think? Some do. I mean, after all, the self-help section of most bookstores enjoys a lot of foot traffic. Most however are convinced that their views of a subject are set. It often takes impetus to change our minds; a death, a birth, an accident, something that forces a shift of perspective. It can also be argued that a change in belief can sneak up on us. It appears to pop up from nowhere and that was my experience. As such, I want to understand deconstruction as a means of examining each tenet of a belief structure and determining the genesis of that tenet and its reliability from a logical perspective. I view this as the tearing down of a building in such a manner as to preserve that which is reusable and that which is to be discarded; deconstruction/construction verses demolition.

In many conversations, I am struck by two seemingly opposed viewpoints; that of an easy process and that of a difficult process (as it pertains to deconstruction). Can it be both? I would postulate that yes, it can be both, and this would, of course, depend on several factors: background, level of belief, the reason for initial contemplation, and probably—the most important—personality!

I discussed this recently with several people and was asked why there is so much anger involved. Those to whom I was talking had begun to review their beliefs, asked questions, and decided that there was no reason for the anger. Instead they felt that the situation warranted joy and thankfulness. My response? *Good for you, now shut the hell up and let me be angry!* See it can be both now let us talk about why.

I remember the moment well. I was a passenger in a car, and out of nowhere, a random thought went through my mind. It was quiet, a simple question … *How do you lose something through your actions that you never did anything to attain through your actions?*

I considered it a moment and moved on. I did not stay there and ruminate. I went about my life only to find that at the most awkward moments, the thoughts would return. I realized somewhere along the way that the question stemmed from 2 Corinthians 5:21, "For our sake, he made him to be sin who knew no sin, so that in him we might become the righteousness of God."

Through my interpretation of this verse, Jesus became us so that we could become him. I know that is simplistic, but as I have been told over and over, it is supposed to be simple. What I found, however, as I examined the idea, it is far from simple and brings about emotional responses depending upon with whom you discuss it. My questions surrounded the idea that I did not ask

God to do this for me, but he did it anyway and I was the recipient of this gift. I did nothing to "become righteousness," yet I was righteous. How then, do I go back to unrighteousness because of anything I would or could do? I digress, but the point is that I did not ask for this question or the resulting mind-bending ruminations that came after. It just happened!

I have had many conversations about deconstruction. There are those that feel it is a negative thing and unnecessary in the flow of belief. There are those that feel it is vital in the growth of an individual. Much of the discourse centers on the idea that deconstruction brings a person to a place of no belief at all. If I were to share my thoughts on that kind of process, I would call it destruction—as in there are no usable, valuable ideas left within the belief system. However, that is not how I see it.

While I do question much of my beliefs pertaining to God and Christianity, I do believe there is value in much of the traditional ideas. Deconstruction, for me, applies to taking something apart, reviewing each piece as to its value, and discarding or saving as makes sense. Additionally, part of deconstruction is a reconstructive process that begins to put things back together. All the saved pieces are picked up, dusted off, and placed ever so carefully back into the overall position.

The danger in all of this is two-fold. I can become dogmatic in my approach. If I have gone through the process of deconstructing my beliefs and coming to a place of new understanding only to decide that I alone have the totality of truth, I have unfortunately set myself up for the process, and the pain, once again. Conversely, I am capable as well of abandoning the process as it seems it will never end. There is a tension between the two that seems correct. Maybe the answers are to occasionally set it all aside and allow my mind to evaluate freely only to then decide I believe something. This is a continual process; not one that ever comes to an end. Just typing that makes me feel exhausted!

> "In deconstruction, to be under way is neither a matter of following a well-marked way, nor a matter of setting out on more uncharted forest paths. Rather it is a matter of following paths that have been so heavily traveled that there is a confusing plethora of tracks and we are not sure whose steps are whose" (Caputo, 2007, p. 49).

NONES AND DONES

> "I was not looking for a perfect church.
> I was looking for an authentic one."
> RICHARD JACOBSEN, *UNCHURCHING*

Several years ago, I came across a book that caught my eye based on the title, "Church Refugees." I was very aware of my own questions at that point and felt as though I might be the only one. (I know it is early for a sidebar, but it is my contention that for all the wonderful talk of loving our enemies and doing for those in need, much of Christianity is somewhat narcissistic. We are constantly focused on ourselves and if we are good enough). So, my assumption that I was on my own, while farfetched, was, nevertheless, how I felt. The title of the book caught my eye, but once I read the book jacket, I was hooked. Apparently, while I was so busy working out my salvation, a lot of people had started asking the same questions I had rolling around in my head. The questions included the relevancy of the church in society: Were we making a difference? Am I the only that feels a commitment to more than the building? Why didn't I feel like I mattered in the grand scheme of all that is the institutionalized church? The real draw to me, however, was that the book was centered around a sociological idea that was dealt with in a scientific manner. While somewhat anecdotal, it was for all intents and purposes, a technical book.

The book uses terms such as "de-churched" or "Dones" as in, "These people are done with the church. They are tired, they are dissatisfied with the structure, the social message, and the politics of the institutional church." Ding, ding, ding ... we have a winner. I could raise my hand for any of those reasons but resoundingly, the business-like political atmosphere within the building was enough to make me grind my teeth. I hated it! The idea of leaving my church was not one I actively sought. If I am honest, it started as exhaustion. I was so busy and "plugged in" to so many ministries and activities, that I could not relax.

To add a level of difficulty to an already problematic situation, I am an introvert. Most do not believe me when I share that little tid bit, but I am most assuredly introverted. I can work a room. I can engage in conversation with almost anyone and find common ground, I have spoken in front of small and large groups alike as well as having sung in front of thousands, but the inner turmoil is not pretty. I need space and quiet. I need to be left alone but when one works in the church, those moments are rare in my experience. Even my kids know and understand that if I am wringing my hands, I am about to freak out.

When I began to doubt my place in the grand scheme, I assumed I needed a rest. What I did not understand at the time was that my thoughts were more focused on whether what I was doing was having a positive impact on those around me and most specifically, on those outsides of my church family. I gave money (tithes and offerings), yet I saw very little of that going into anything other than rent on the building and the pastor's salary ... and before you ask, yes, I did the books, so I know where the money went.

When new people came to our church, they typically were transplants, not the "world" we were hoping to touch. Who were we feeding? Who were we healing or helping to heal? Were we even generous to those seeking help that managed to find the building? Honestly, one of my biggest pet peeves was that those coming for help were told that they must participate in the church to receive any kind of assistance. Although I do understand the reasoning, it always left a bad taste in my mouth. These are *my* reasons, but many of those identifying as a "Done" expressed these same types of problems as well.

I kept looking for God and would, of course, feel as though he were in the building during service, but I did not see much of His presence outside the doors. I wanted to be that presence; I wanted to be his hands and feet, but I was continually reminded that people were best served inside the building. The continual need for more people, bigger buildings, more programs, all became exhausting. I could only hear so many times that we were not friendly enough, accommodating enough, did not love people enough before I had to ask a question. *What was the end game?* I mean even if we were able to accomplish all those things to the level suggested and resulted in numerous people entering, what were we hoping to achieve? I already knew the answer on a couple different levels. The primary one was that we were getting people saved, but the secondary was that the more people committing to the church, the more tithing/donations, the better the church was able to meet its financial responsibilities. That turns my stomach.

So, let's talk about that for a moment. I have come across many different attitudes about those who choose not to attend church. In one recent conversation in which the term "the Dones" was discussed, one gentleman on Facebook made the following point:

> "The term 'Done' seems to denote those who have been harmed by the church, for which the church rightfully stands indicted and should repent. But also, "Done" seems to denote those who don't like to get up on Sunday mornings and commit themselves to being held accountable for their discipleship. It's the old, "I love Jesus but hate religion" attitude that forgets that Jesus came to them through a particular set of practices called religion and a particular people called the Church."

I find the idea that people just do not want to get out of bed to be somewhat shallow...the quote supposes that you are either really hurt, bitter, or lazy. There is so much more to understanding a large phenomenon that is happening in the church. (Please note when I use the word "church," I am not referring to the building but the body. The two are not the same.) How did we get to this place in which people are supposed bitter or lazy because they choose not to enter a building? How have we moved past the Ekklesia and decided that meeting in the same place on the same day each week fits the definition. Don't get me wrong, those doing so may be engaging in Ekklesia, but that is often not the case. I have said repeatedly that religious and spiritual relationships based on the building are convenient but not necessarily real.

Religious circles are not the only place this change occurs. The retail industry is experiencing a shift due to an increased internet presence. Let's face it, we can do almost everything online now, and as I previously introduced myself as an introvert, this is a perfect situation for me. However, this idea does not go over well as it pertains to spirituality and fellowship. Don't get me wrong, most churches are now participating on the internet to bring their brand of spirituality and ethics into the homes of people. There is a wide array of books available for download on demand, podcasts too numerous to count, and even small church pastors are making their sermons available on websites via video and audio recording.

I personally love having it all at my disposal, but I can honestly see that it could have diminishing effects on the traditional church setting. I have been informed numerous times, that regardless of the availability of such resources, I am still expected to be in church for the "fellowship." That word seems to be a holy grail for those who espouse an expectation to attend a building. Just try to make the argument that "fellowship" can happen in various ways, and you will hear that it just isn't the same. I know this because I have been reminded how important it is to attend a building. I could, in all snarky honesty, accept this much better if those demanding it were not receiving a paycheck from their church. I know, I'm jaded! In all seriousness though, the idea of fellowship at a specific building is one that I find problematic. It is almost rote! Just show up at a building once a week (or more in some cases), see the same people, ask the same questions, blah, blah, blah. These is no work involved for the relationship. It is one of convenience! Try leaving the building and see how many of those "friends" maintain a relationship. It takes work to be in fellowship with one another. You must go out of your way to maintain communication and input into one another's lives.

Perhaps one of the biggest complaints I have heard is that of relevance. Many want to know how the things that are being taught within the physical religious setting applies out in the "real world."

For example, how does one reconcile the persistence of people living with hunger while purchasing a new sound system? After all, we are instructed to feed the poor. How does one reconcile "loving your enemies" and then deal with the ugly vitriol that seems to find its way to the surface of any political discussion? Yes, even in church? There are probably hundreds of similar questions that can be asked. So what is one to do and maybe, even more importantly, how do we deal with the conflicting emotions evoked by such belief-oriented questions? Maybe the best way to sum up my questions is the following:

> "They wanted community and they got judgment. They wanted to affect the life of the church and they got bureaucracy. They wanted conversation and they got doctrine. They wanted meaningful engagement with the world, and they got moral prescription."

I felt all of this. Every day, I could see injustice in the local and world news. I saw people hurting, starving, enduring war and all kinds of abuse. Where was the church in all of this? I needed to know that I was making a difference. I did not hate God or my church family. I did not want to shame an institution. I wanted to see it rise to the level of expectation that one has for a moral and ethical organization. I wanted to see the ethics of Jesus at work. I do believe most have good intentions but somewhere along the way, we get lost in the details and forget the bigger mandate.

Another issue within the church is that of an obligation to service. The obligation is held out as a calling by God to a specific area. The following example was told to me in a conversation about ministry and how that applies to everyday life.

"I understand about being in my 40's having little income and never having a house of my own. I spent the years I should have been building a career so involved in church, outreaches and at times fulltime ministry, that I had no time to look out for my own well-being. I am grateful for some of the experiences, but often feel that I was really building a person's kingdom more than God's. And the people I spent so much time loving and supporting and neglecting my self-care, are no better off now than they were before. I know that we do not do the things to get back, and I do not ever regret love and giving of myself, but I wish I would have been more wise and built something for me and my future daughter, instead of being so gung-ho to save the world and to try to bear the burdens of ministry and church leaders, people in the church and even the community. I'm 41, never owned a house, still working on my education to have a job I love that both helps people and helps me pay my bills and give my daughter a good education."

Part of the issue is that we have all been conditioned that we must have a ministry and win souls to Christ. There are thousands of students studying ministry work in Christian colleges who are going to end up broke and disillusioned, wondering why. Loving God has no such requirement. Walking with Christ means, hand-in-hand, in the everyday stillness that is life.

I read an article recently that stated financial figures for a well-known Christian school. No accreditation, no job training, just ministry. They bring in $7 million annually. For what? The expectation of having some big ministry and influencing people. We've all felt that pull. I've been there. I've been told I'm meant to lead people and speak into people's lives. I've lived with some large expectation and the complete physical, emotional, and spiritual exhaustion that comes along with it. I worked my ass off and finally realized that the calling to be a pastor is not a call of vocation but a call of the heart. We've made it a profession, but it is really a personal endeavor; it's about caring for people. It will never make you rich, but it may very well help someone else in their need. I am a pastor, not because I need the label (and don't use it by the way), but because my heart is for people.

Do what you love. Help people as you find them in the everyday walk of life if you can. Be a voice of support and love, acceptance and mercy. And if somewhere along the way, you wander into a building, it's all good, but ministry happens where the people are, and many people refuse to go there.

In all the reading I have done, over and over, I find that those identifying as "Done" are not actually done with God as many might suspect or accuse. Rather, they are done with the broken system. They seek true spirituality. They want the broken system made right, and in many cases, they identify with the broken people. Let's be honest … there is a large section of society that identifies itself as Christian yet appears nothing like Christ. Even if it is your belief that the secular world is lost, they aren't stupid and can see blatant hypocrisy.

I absolutely confess to willingly being a part of the system of expectation and almost corporate like atmosphere. We are raised on the ideas of faithfully following. We are raised to believe in complete capitulation and allegiance to God. But what happens when you begin to see your beliefs in opposition to who God is or should be?

Simple personal example: I wanted to travel and involve myself in the lives of those around the world. I wanted to minister to those that had never heard of Jesus. I heard endlessly that it had to be God's will and He would make a way *if* I was intended to do what my heart felt.

I waited years. *Years.* I was called on by those in church leadership to pray for others to go, provided financial assistance and means for many others to go, but it never occurred to me that I could just go.

It was not until I was out of the building that I decided to do just that … go! I did not ask permission. I did not wait for God to provide the financial and emotional assistance (although I did have some who helped me). I did not wait for the right circumstances, nor did I wait for those who were "supposed" to go with me. I just went! It was one of the best experiences of my life. I did not preach, teach, or minister. I simply went and learned about the culture and the people living there. I shared my experiences when asked including those of my belief system. I was scared to go but faced that fear and found peace. Now, I know someone is thinking that it was finally God's timing. Maybe that is true, but if so, his timing coincided with me losing my patience with a system that holds people back more than it pushes them forward.

So, much can be ascertained from the perspective of those leaving the traditional institutional church, but what of the other "side"? Those administering the church? One attitude I have come across when interacting with clergy is that of disbelief. The clergy simply do not believe church attendance is dwindling. Others give excuses such as population growth outpacing church attendance thereby skewing the percentages. To be fair, I know of several pastors that have embraced the cultural shift and encourage home fellowships and local outreach. They want to see people being the church more than going to church. However, in my experience they are the minority.

Most have doubled down on religious rhetoric about failure to fellowship and the idea of accountability. I have literally been told that I am unfaithful to God because I do not attend a building. On one occasion, it was decided that I was a false teacher because I did not *demand* that people attend church. The same person went on to ask me to let him know "how sulfur smelled." There's that Christian love. On my snarkier days, I will retort that my former pastor must then accept at least some of that responsibility as I did not ask to leave, but that is only when I am feeling particularly raw and hurt.

HOW I WAS SHOVED OFF THE CLIFF OF DECONSTRUCTION

"Change in life is inevitable even if not always comfortable. Oftentimes, we fight it as it brings up fears that we hold or exposes feelings in us that we wish to keep hidden. Regardless of the reasons that we avoid change, most are not looking to run to the next big thing. We will, if necessary, make those small adjusting course corrections and feel pretty good about our ability to roll with the punches. What happens though when the rug is pulled out from under us? How do we respond when all of life seems to shift at the same moment? For most, and most decidedly for me, I dig my heels in and feel like I have to diligently hold my position, you know, be the warrior of faith and believe that if I resist long enough, those changes will flee. The truth however is God often institutes those changes. He sets a seemingly new course and asks us to check the prevailing winds. This can be quite a shock to the system. I have a daughter that played softball from the age of seven through college (I know it seems like I changed subjects but stay with me for a moment). There were times when we had been traveling a while and she was playing almost constantly that she would tire and begin to struggle with her performance at the plate. Her batting average would suffer even though the mechanics were there. This produced a sense of frustration in her and often an attitude. I would give her time to work it out and make the adjustments that would be beneficial. Often, though, I would have to step in and grab her by the ponytail, pull her close to me and in clipped tones tell her that her attitude was wearing on me. I would tell her to change which side of the plate she was batting from or try bunting instead of hitting away—anything to readjust her eye and focus. There were times when a whole new team was necessary to change the frustration and move on to where she was trying to get. Usually this would anger her, and I would endure a period of time in which she pouted or ignored me. Within due time, she would come to me and thank me for reminding her of the need to change the focus sometimes. As I relate this, I am reminded that she is much like me. I sometimes feel angry or frustrated and God has to yank my ponytail and suggest I refocus! After almost a year of struggling with my thoughts and allowing God to show me more of Him, He asked something big! He asked my husband and I along with our family to step away from what has been our home spiritually for 16 years. Yesterday was our last day with our church family. I would like to say that I recognized it right away, but the truth is that God had to kick us pretty hard in order to exact the change. We do not make those kinds of changes easily. It was an extremely emotional day for me. Everyone wants to know why. I do not have those answers readily available or in totality. There are always those things that you could point to as excuses and even pile numerous examples together, but the truth is they were just the catalyst. The actual reason is that God said, "Get out of your country ... .and go to a place that I will show you." I will remember fondly those moments of fellowship and learning along with a lot of experiences. I will endeavor to continue in those relationships that mean so much to me all the while remembering that we are the body of Christ, the real meaning of the word "church" and no matter where we are, we are one body. God has asked for the next phase to begin. I want to press toward the goal. I want the prize of the upward call! While my jaw is still sore from rolling with the latest punch, I know that God is leading and because of that, I can make the change."

I wrote the above section the day following my last day in church. I was hurting, angry and confused but more than anything, I was numb. The previous few years had taken a toll on my Christian perspective and the final straw of being kicked out of my church family pushed me to a place that felt and still feels like a wilderness. We have all heard of the desert experience of the Israelites. Well, my desert is just as dry and lonely.

So, I want to explain the circumstances that led me to my deconstruction. This is not to say that this was the very beginning but rather, was the push that sent me over the edge. I am going to do my best to recall and share my experience without speaking to the supposed motives of those involved (I said I would do my best!). Honestly, it would not be fair of me to share my thoughts on the motives involved without allowing for rebuttal. Suffice it to say that I was systematically questioned, accused, and dismissed by someone who had been my best friend for over a decade.

I have mentioned elsewhere that not everyone has a slow, smooth slide into questioning their belief system. For some, myself included, the process happens in the wake of a painful situation. It is jarring and shocking! The foundation falls out from under you and you find yourself flat on your back looking up and wondering if you can get up or if you should even try.

Now, you may question why I was reserved in my writing above after such a painful separation and that would be a fair question. Why not just unleash with both barrels and skewer those who hurt me? I wanted to—you have no idea—but I had personal responsibility and good Christian behavior pounded into me from early childhood. What I wrote was for public consumption and, in my mind, I believed that I would maintain relationships with those that remained in my church family. What I found was that it was just in my mind.

About a year prior to leaving, a verse popped into my mind. We have all heard the verse but for some reason it would not stop running through my brain and into my consciousness. Day and night, it seemed to follow me everywhere. When I was finally disturbed enough to ask someone for their opinion, it was really something that I believed I was supposed to understand. As such, I was fairly adamant in my questioning.

My husband and I often had dinner or just socialized at our pastor's house. The pastor and his wife were our closest friends. Our kids dated one another, spent major holidays together, and even joked about growing old as friends and sharing rocking chairs. We were close, so it was in their living room one evening that I asked my question. I recited the verse that was prompting the questions and shared how relentless the question felt to me. If you recall from my description of growing up, I was always trying to be good enough and keep God happy. I had never verbalized it, but I was squarely in the camp of those who believe you can lose your salvation. The idea of losing my salvation and un-becoming God's righteousness was so troubling to me terrified me growing up and even deep into my adulthood. So, I asked my question, "How can I lose something or un-become something that I never did anything to become?"

The room fell quiet for what felt like a long time, but then everyone spoke. Strangely, or maybe not so strangely, no one addressed my actual question. Instead, I was repeatedly reminded that there was still sin, and we were still sinners. I actually attempted to push back a few times and try to return the conversation to my actual question, but finally, realized I was not going to get an answer. The closest I came to an answer was when my friend and my pastor suggested that when we did not understand something, we should just ignore it and "put it on a shelf" until such a time as an answer presented itself. The exchange left me feeling unsatisfied, and I was honest about that feeling. I explained that as the question would not leave me alone, I did not think that ignoring it was going to work, nor was I interested in doing so. The evening continued, the subject was changed, and we went on as though it had not happened.

In hindsight, I should have said something to the effect of: "If you do not know or have an answer, that is perfectly acceptable, I will search elsewhere." I have no issue with someone not knowing the answer; after all, I did not know either. In reality, the subject was closed, but it was at the point that I began to look at theological articles, read books of differing belief structures within Christianity, listen to podcasts and sermons from other preachers. Basically, I started hunting for my answer. The problem with doing this is that you do not wind up with answers, just more questions … many more questions.

Over the next year and a half, I read so many books, attended conferences, took classes, and built new relationships all while maintaining my responsibilities at my home church. There is an adage that 80% of the work in a church is done by 20% of the people. Well, I definitely fell into the 20%. I was preaching, ran a discipleship school and taught courses. I was a worship leader, nursery worker (just because), prayer team partner with my husband, and a prophet (per the pastor himself). That should have been my first clue that something was coming. After all, a prophet is not without honor except in his own town, among his own relatives, and in his own home.

All the things I was learning were becoming a part of what I spoke about. My views changed, and I discovered grace. At that time, I felt I had come to the totality of truth. This was it ... I finally understood grace, or so I thought, but it was not well received. I mean we talked a good game at our church about grace being what saved us, but in the words of Brennen Manning, "Put bluntly, the American church today accepts grace in theory but denies it in practice. We say we believe that the fundamental structure of reality is grace, not works—but our lives refute our faith. By and large, the gospel of grace is neither proclaimed, understood, or lived."

Ironically, it had been my friend and pastor who said I was too hard on myself and needed to understand grace. Looking back, I realize he meant I needed to understand his definition of grace because mine just got me accused of demonic oppression. Yes, I am serious!

As I said, what I was learning about grace emerged in how I taught and in the way I prayed for people. I had quite a few in my classes who had life changing realizations. Marriages were improving, identities were becoming realized, flowers were growing, birds were singing ... oops, sorry, I got carried away for a moment. In all seriousness though, I was seeing for the first time what grace, mercy, and love could do not only in my life but in the lives of those around me. It was incredible and everything that I had always believed a relationship with God was supposed to be.

Soon, I noticed my pastor standing in the back of the room while I was teaching classes. I really did not think much of it at first, but after a while, I could see he was frowning. It confused me because I was teaching from a curriculum that he had chosen. I was actually pretty careful to not bring in too much of what I was independently reading and learning unless it could be supported by my understanding of scripture and that which I thought would be acceptable in my church. (Side bar—that makes it sound as though I had some wild ideas, but in reality, I was just cautious because I did not trust myself to internalize what I was reading and discussing with others). While all of this was going on over the last year or so, people had been transitioning out of our church. I know it happens, but there always seemed to be some drama associated with the departure. Of course, I only knew one side of the issue. I was in leadership, and my husband was on the church board. We knew almost everything that happened, but we did not ask questions because that felt like gossip.

As time went on though, the exodus was more noticeable and closer to us in who was leaving. We were much more aware of both "sides." There was growing dissent against the pastor personally and in the way the church was being managed. Multiple conversations among the board members became heated, and it was not long before one member announced that he and his family were leaving. I leave out the church politics and other details, but it was evident to many, my husband and I included, that our pastor was acting differently.

I am empathetic, whether it be in a crowd or specifically with individuals. I internalize emotions, and so the closer this brewing situation came to me, the less I was able to remain silent. Eventually, I reached a point at which I requested a one-on-one meeting with our pastor. I sat in his office and asked if he was okay. He assured me he was, but as one of my best friends, I knew something was off. I broached the subject of congregation members leaving as well as some concerns that others within the church had brought to my attention.

I was actually shocked at his response. His explanation to me was that he had a church to run and did not have time for people, their demands, or their problems. It almost felt like an apathetic business meeting. He explained that his role was like that of an engineer on a train: if the train cars start leaving the tracks, he just needed to pull harder and they would straighten out.

I sat, shocked. How could he not care about *why* his "train cars" were coming off the track. I suggested this was a wrongly skewed way of viewing the situation and asked how that stacked up with the example Jesus provided of the lost sheep. After all, the shepherd left the 99 and in search of the one. The one mattered. The shepherd cared. In this case, it was more than just one; it was many, and I could not understand what was happening. I left his office that day feeling on edge and, quite frankly, angry.

One of the larger agendas for my church at that time was initiating some form of ministry in India. Our pastor had some contacts there, and a decision had been made to begin training a team to relocate to India on a long-term basis. My son-in-law (before he was my son-in-law) accompanied the pastor on a trip to India to "plant seeds" and gauge what to expect.

The trip went well, and the expectation was that my daughter and her soon-to-be husband, would marry and then become our missionaries in India. It made sense. She previously participated in several trips for missionary purposes. Her fiancé had lived a year in Ecuador as well as some small trips working in a missionary capacity. My husband and I were understandably nervous, but we just kept believing this was God's will...except that I did not truly believe that it was. I was struggling! Everything felt "off" not only with the idea of missions, but in general. There was administrative and vocal unrest in the church, and many had already abandoned the church family.

As I mentioned before, I felt restless and out of place and had so for some time. I was told that I was supposed to be a pastor and have an office down the hall, but I inwardly cringed at the thought. I believed something was wrong with *me* for having doubts, but more issues continually surfaced that seemed wrong. I did not have a reason, so in true Christian evangelical style, I assumed the devil was attacking me. (Sidebar: One thing I've noticed is that often the devil is a scapegoat for everything going wrong, meaning you have to dig in and resist. The problem with that mindset is that it leaves no room for the possibility that you could just be wrong!)

Several concerns were introduced by the board regarding the India endeavor. The safety of the missionaries was a significant issue as the designated mission field was close to the Pakistani border. The logistics of establishing housing and support posed additional problems. We were a pretty small church, roughly no more than 100 people at any given time, so the idea that we could commit to such an undertaking was difficult to comprehend. I just kept praying, because that is what a good Christian woman does, right? We pray! Except I have never on my best day been a good Christian woman, and I just kept trying to figure out why I was doubting. I trusted those making the decisions would seek guidance from God, but I could not shake my doubts. I should mention that I struggled quite a bit with self-confidence. I never believed that I was hearing God correctly. If I "gave a word" in church, I almost had to choke before I would speak. Then, afterward, I would torture myself, doubting what I heard. I had no problems believing that others heard God, so I remained silent and struggled.

Several months later, I drove home from church with my daughter. We chatted about the mission plans. As I was not in the meetings with those involved in the planning, nor was I involved in the board meetings, I asked her what she thought about everything. She shared some of the ideas as well as timeline details. While this was good to know, in the middle of the conversation, I just asked, "How do you feel about going?"

She quieted for a moment and then began to cry. I quickly pulled over, asking what was wrong. She admitted she was not sure she should go but felt so much pressure. They assumed she committed because her fiancé was going. So, in true Christian fashion, I asked her what she thought God was saying. Her answer almost made me throw up. She replied that she hadn't heard from God that she was supposed to go to India, but the pastor told her that he had heard from God and this was what she was supposed to do. I was so angry, I actually yelled for a few minutes allowing all my doubts and frustration to pour out. So instead of those involved encouraging her to explore her feelings and make a sound decision, they led her to believe she was wrong and did not hear God … about India, about her thoughts, feelings…about her life! I am honestly angry all over again just thinking about it.

Once we got home, my husband and I sat down with her and asked questions. I told her that her apprehension was valid and maybe was God telling her no. Regardless, our position was: if you do not feel comfortable, you are not doing it! She actually did have a conversation with her fiancé who was squarely on her side (he should be) and the pastor. While there was disappointment, they agreed more time was necessary before the planning continued. So, problem solved, right? Not really, it seemed to bleed into more issues with disagreement and loyalty.

Maybe it was my imagination, but after this course of events, things began to slide downhill. I felt more and more uncomfortable. Numerous people came to me and shared their doubts about staying at our church. I was literally receiving text messages in the middle of services and fielding questions in my classes regarding concerning issues like teaching from the pulpit and other church family members that were no longer welcome to attend. I had no idea how to respond. I felt loyalty to my pastor, my best friend, yet shared the concerns with the direction the church was going. I brought up the subject several more times and tried to gently address the issues that seemed to be the center of concern, but I received aggravated responses and a desire to know *who exactly* was unhappy.

In hindsight, two separate events ended up breaking my relationship with my best friend. As I previously mentioned, my husband was on the church board, so we received an invitation along with the other board members to a dinner. Membership was not expanding as hoped, so several previous attempts of bringing advisors to address logistics failed as identified problems were never considered important enough to correct. We had repeatedly heard that we needed to grow and that we needed to uncover the underlying causes as to why it was not happening. However, as aforementioned, findings were dismissed as frivolous and unfounded. It really did begin to resemble a business and the meetings seemed to be problem solving conference room meetings.

A pastor from the East Coast was invited for the weekend, wanting to meet with church leadership. I was invited to that Friday evening's dinner, but, in all honesty, I did not want to go. It had been a long week for me. I was tired and not really interested in discussion. It had been my contention for a while that we should be preaching Jesus and letting Him build the church. I mean, everyone says that but then still tries to find ways to influence people. I convinced myself, prior to this dinner, that I just needed to stay quiet. I was not in the best mood or even in the best place spiritually to converse about the topic. So, I ate dinner and behaved … for as long as I could. Let's be honest, anyone who knows me would have been shocked that I remained quiet for as long as I had. I literally put my hand over my mouth several times during the evening.

Finally, the visiting pastor sat on a stool in front of us and began to explain what his reasoning behind our lack of church growth. To this day, I am still confused as to why someone from across the country felt that he knew us and our church well enough to be so blunt. I am sure he had conversations with our pastor before that night, but there is no way that he had an unbiased view. He proceeded to state that we were at fault for people failing to come to our church. We were not committed enough or involved enough … and on it went. Honestly, by this time I felt like I was going to have a stroke holding my tongue, and I must have made some kind of face or a noise because he looked right at me and asked what I thought about his ideas. I did try to control my response. I took a deep breath and said, "I disagree." He wanted to know with what I disagreed, so I went on to tell him that I did not feel he was in a position to make these observations. Further, I could not care any less about the number of butts in our seats. His reaction was so cartoon-like. His eyes widened, and he almost fell off the stool. I continued that until we were more concerned about the people outside the building and meeting them where they were, our priorities were out-of-line.

To say the room was quiet is an understatement. I was keenly aware of the pastors in the room and could feel the tension pulsate. I could have predicted his response … We had to get people in the building in order to affect them and that my response was indicative of the problem. The meeting ended not long after that. I shut up again and waited to leave. I received some communication later from some of the other attendees thanking me for speaking up, but no one publicly condoned my actions and there was not one word from the pastor.

The second event was several months later. It was a Sunday morning, and I was on the schedule to help lead worship. I was in the building early for practice and was sitting in the sanctuary waiting for the musicians to set up. At one point, the pastor approached me and asked to speak with me in his office when we were done rehearsing. I am not sure how many have had this experience, but it was like a weight pressed on my shoulders because I knew what it was about. The previous week, I was on the worship team and during a quieter moment was compelled to speak what I felt God was wanting to say to the congregation. This was not a new thing. I had literally been doing this for years and was always nervous about doing so for the reason I explained earlier ... self-doubt. But this time, the moment I began to speak, the worship leader of the week strummed his guitar louder. This of course is the internationally known cue that you are bringing the chorus of the song back around again. I continued, and within a few seconds, the worship leader realized what was happening and backed off. No big deal, right? Except that I knew immediately that it was. No one mentioned it and several people approached me after service to share that the "word" was exactly what they needed to hear. So, now, I was sitting in the same sanctuary a week later knowing that I had to answer for the *faux pas*.

Once practice was over, I left for the office. We had gone a little longer in our preparation so there was only about 15 minutes until the service was to begin. As such, I asked if he still wanted to talk or wait until afterward. He assured me it would not take long and had me sit across his desk from him. (Remember when I said I would not assign motive? Well … .it is my contention that this was to remind me who was in charge but that is only my opinion.) He proceeded to tell me that I had been out of order the previous week, and I thought he meant I had given an incorrect word. This was always my biggest fear and he knew that. He was my best friend; we had had these discussions many times. When I asked what was wrong with the word, he assured me it had been fine, but his contention was that I had stepped outside biblical order for the service. Now that was confusing because he was referencing scripture from Paul about orderly service and interpretation, yet the word was given without need for interpretation. I pointed out that I did not understand how it was out of order. After stumbling around for a short time, he told me that I had spoken over the worship leader's playing, that the leader had been going in another direction. I was still confused and clarified once again that there was nothing wrong with the word. He agreed again that it was fine, but that I had not listened to the Holy Spirit for the timing. I asked if it was possible that the worship leader had not listened to the Holy Spirit. He conceded to the possibility but then, at that point, directed my attention to the time, indicating we needed to start the service. He hoped I understood what needed to be done differently.

This little talk upset me quite a bit. Every ounce of self-doubt I had screamed in my head. I felt horrible and embarrassed, yet still confused. I was so upset that I could not sing during service. I stood with the worship team but just stepped back from the microphone, closed my eyes and waited for it to be over. I did not say a word to anyone about it, and as I was visibly upset, I left the sanctuary and worked in the nursery for the remainder of the service. Later that day after returning home, my husband inquired as to what had been wrong. He knew something was but had no idea what had transpired. I offered some weak excuses but, in the end, told him about the conversation. Upset, he wanted to discuss the situation, but because I was struggling, I just wanted to let it go. I would get over it, move forward.

Eventually, he spoke with the pastor as a friend, explaining to him that he had hurt my feelings and that I was now struggling with doubt. To say the least, the message wasn't well received. A few days later, I received an email from my pastor telling me that he could not believe that I was afraid to come talk with him. My pride bolstered me to respond that I was not afraid, and I would be happy to meet with him. It was not a pleasant discussion. Upon further conversation, he reiterated that I had been out of line, that the worship leader had heard the Holy Spirit, and I just needed to move on. I had to laugh a bit because that was what I had decided to do before he asked to discuss it some more.

Looking back, I know that he was not happy and probably threatened that I challenged him on the biblical mandate of order. Further, I suggested that he was adding his own understanding to the text in order to control a situation. Did I mention that I can be mouthy and that I have a bad temper? I have found that challenging "men of God" can have bad results and that was certainly what happened. One thing that stood out to me was a comment related to his relationship with the worship leader. He was somewhat newer at leading, and the pastor had mentioned several times that they had lunch together and that he was helping him. During this conversation, he made mention that he had been in the ear of the worship leader; therefore, the worship leader's timing was correct. It was while he was referencing the lunches and what not that suddenly I understood what he was saying. Our church did not use monitors on the stage. We had begun using a new sound system that allowed each participant to use ear buds and control the sound of the instruments and other vocals in their ear. It helped alleviate the constantly challenging dilemma of "I cannot hear myself." Each vocal and instrument was on a separate channel as was the pastor's microphone apparently. So, when he mentioned being "in the worship leader's ear," he was referring to the open channel from his microphone that spoke directly to the worship leader. He had been calling the shots for the worship session when I began speaking that day. Once I understood this, I asked why he needed to do so. His response was that he was teaching the worship leader to follow the Holy Spirit. I've already confessed to being somewhat of a smartass, so it should come as no surprise that I could not resist saying, "It sounds like he is learning to follow you." Probably not the best thing to say in retrospect, but I did, and quite honestly, I finally understood what I had done out of order … I had spoken over the pastor. Wait, is that in scripture? After that, we did not speak much except for polite hellos and goodbyes. I waited a bit and finally sent an email apologizing if I had upset him or hurt him. I missed my friend and wanted to fix things. I never received a response, so I sent another email asking for forgiveness and a chance to discuss and resolve our feelings. I did receive a reply to that one suggesting that I was mistaken and that he was more sure of his direction than ever before. He stated that he disagreed with everything in my previous email and was not interested in going over it again. My intent was not to belabor the issue but to bring healing to the relationship, but he just insisted that it was not necessary. He did say that maybe we should meet since my email had "a hint of finality" to it. I am still unsure of what finality he was referencing, but I did realize the relationship had shifted and would not be the same going forward.

In the midst of all of this, my husband and two other board members resigned as they were uncomfortable with some of the direction of the church and the board. I should mention that the bylaws of the church were written in such a fashion as to allow the pastor to move forward with board approval and that had never been an issue in the past. However, with the church business model and the India issues, questions were arising, and there was not full agreement on the board. Provisions in the bylaws gave the board members the ability to access an outside accountability group if problems were found within the church. This had to be done with unanimous approval of the board members other than the pastor. The problem with this was that the pastor had appointed his wife to the board, and she was vocal that only a moral failing would prompt her to vote against her husband. As this seemed to be a conflict of interest, resignations resulted. So, on a Sunday after church, my husband tendered his resignation. The following Wednesday, we received an email informing us that we would be leaving, and that next Sunday would be our last. We were told that we would be "prayed out", meaning that we would be put in front of the congregation and prayed for as we exited. We were thanked for our years of service and time at the church along with blessings and wishes for our prosperity.

We had not decided to leave; we were trying to determine what was happening and what we should do. I have replayed the whole scenario over and over for a long time. Looking back, I would have done some things differently, but nothing that would have changed the outcome. I just shut down after that. I think I have gone to church no more than five times since then. I cannot make it make sense. Even, my children were sent packing. Apparently, God no longer called them to India.

Not too long ago, I asked my husband if I misread the situation. Did we decide to leave or were we dismissed? He confirmed that I am remembering it correctly—we were dismissed. Not only did we lose our place of worship, but we lost our best friends. To this day, no one from that church contacts us nor associates with us. If we see them around town, it is awkward and tense. We all do the right thing; we smile and ask how one another is doing, but it is obviously superficial. Devastating!

It still hurts! I am still angry and heartbroken. My older daughter was away at college when all of this took place and has not been as affected. She still goes to church. My husband attends a church most weeks and jokes about "going to get saved." My younger daughter, both my sons, and myself do not attend. To some extent, we have all been broken in the process. I am probably the most vocal having talked more about it, but there is damage across the board. I felt a huge amount of responsibility. It appeared I was the one seeking answers to supposedly dangerous questions. I was the one who aggressively pushed back. I was the one who initiated conversation on difficult subjects. I was the one who refused to back down.

My husband told me many times that I may have led the way, but they were right behind me. Sometimes that helps, but other times I just feel like I was the one driving the car in a wreck that damaged everyone. Trying to understand my beliefs as well as the interpersonal relationships aspect has been daunting. The doubt remains. The questions never end. I have had to make as much peace with uncertainty as I can. The truth is that I struggled with what I believed long before I was shown the door, but I assumed I would have my friends on that journey.

It took me a while to understand that I was grieving and even longer to see that others in this process are as well. Once I did, however, it helped to realize that this is a natural thing. When we begin to examine what we believe, there is an evolution, and there are regrets. If that process begins because of abuses or traumatic experiences, it can only hurt more. I do believe there are many people struggling with all the emotions of confronting these changes. I am beginning to see that we all need to give ourselves and others time to process the pain of change.

STAGES OF POWER

Within the first few weeks of the life coaching certification course, I was introduced to a book that I immediately bought. It is actually a business book, yet it was so succinct in its description of this process that I had to pay attention. *Real Power*, written by Janet O. Hagberg, outlines a journey of where we each get our "power," and the evolution that we experience between differing stages of power. As I said, it is a business book but so applicable to deconstruction. Additionally, to me it offered a glimpse of why we all seem to be so different in our approaches and places on the spectrum.

The stages she outlines are not necessarily within a short period of time. To me they represented a continuum throughout a lifespan. The primary stage is that of powerlessness. Now anyone can feel powerless depending upon where they are in life, their age, their lack of vocation, or lack of standing in the community. Furthermore, just because one has moved beyond this stage does not mean they will never again experience this feeling.

So, let's think about this stage as it pertains to our closely held belief system. Speaking from a Christian experience, finding Jesus is all about powerlessness. We are encouraged to see ourselves as nothing and in need of a savior. We are, at our very essence, spiritually powerless. Often, we have reached this place as a result of pain or need. While not even understanding why, we reach out to a God in order to ease this sense of helplessness. (Sidebar: Think about how often in Christianity we are reminded of our power through Christ. His very name is used as some sort of invoking power and wielded like a weapon.) Janet goes on to explain that each stage has its "shadow" which describes those attributes of someone who has overstayed their welcome at any particular stage. Shadows of this first stage include addictions or maintaining a victim stance. "What a wretched man I am!" from Romans 7:24, springs to mind for me. The constant need to remind oneself of their inferiority and need of a savior keeps them coming back for more, even if the experience becomes abusive in its application.

The second stage is that of power by association. Who does not like to be around important people? The church ironically is full of Christian celebrities. They exist at every level of the belief structure. I have sat in countless conferences in which those attending just want the opportunity to have a picture taken with the speaker and announce to all on social media that they have met and spoken with said celebrity. I cringe as I type because I am just as guilty.

Those at this stage are basically apprentices to the influential. They are learning the ins and outs of the accepted norms as well as developing a dependence upon those they admire. Now be honest, how many times have we all discovered our next guru, buy every book they published, hope to see them in person or spend a few minutes in their presence? We are impressed. We want association with those that impress. I should probably interject here that there is no inherent negative judgment at any of these stages. They just are a part of the process, so do not read into anything I am saying as a condemnation, especially since I have been there myself and sometimes still reside in any one of these stages. The danger, or shadow, of this stage is that of imitation. While imitation is considered the sincerest form of flattery, in this case, it leads to losing oneself. Shifting your behavior to that of those you follow disallows you to be you. We are each unique in our gifts and talents. Those should never be traded because of a fan boy (or fan girl) crush on a Christian celebrity.

Stage three is one in which people get stuck for a long time, it is the stage of power by achievement. I fully admit that this is one stage that I continually find myself back in. Again, there is nothing inherently wrong with this stage, but it can produce burnout and exhaustion. When this stage was presented to me, I found myself angry, condemned for trying to make myself a better person. It was here that I started questioning my importance and to try to gain importance through pedigree. I needed more education. I need more certifications. I needed to be published ... oh wait, those still are my goals. Again, there is nothing wrong with my goals. It only becomes wrong when I use them to try and prove myself to others, and I have done that. Success is addictive; we all like to feel successful.

When we move from stage two association to stage three success, it finally feels like we have arrived. I have known people over the years yearning for a ministry to call their own. They knew they needed to pay their dues and work within an existing ministry (usually wanting it to be high-profile), but the endgame was always their own deal. Several years ago, I wrote a blog post about this phenomenon. It had occurred to me that often in Christian circles, we are taught that we have a purpose, and as we are charged with sharing the gospel, our purpose must include ministry to others. Not many envision cleaning toilets or cleaning up after church as their ministry. Those actions are the price you pay to get to a ministry. Ironically, however, Adam was not created to have a world-wide ministry but rather to have a relationship with God. So, why do we work ourselves to stress and bad health to prove we are valuable? So, any guesses as to the shadow side of stage three? It should come as no surprise that those feeling powerful by way of achievement can become egocentric. Their ministry is *their* ministry. It does not belong to God but is their gift to God and as such, they must look good doing it.

Greed is another shadow response. The ministry is never big enough or influential enough. It must grow and exceed any other ministry. I sat in a service at one point in which the pastor announced from the pulpit that he was going to India. Nothing so earth shattering about that announcement, except that his wife found out at the same time as the congregants. He had a whole ministry dynamic worked out, and it was going to be grand. It did not seem to matter that he did not include personal support system. Ask me if it ever happened … nope, not as of this writing.

Are you tired yet? Here is where it starts getting good. Stage four involves the idea of power by reflection. For me, this is where deconstruction begins. You have done the powerless game, then met many of your mentors, attended conferences, and started your own ministries. Suddenly, none of it feels satisfying anymore. Something is off. I read Rob Bell's book *Velvet Elvis* (and loved it by the way). In this book, he discusses when things started to feel off to him. He had created this amazing mega church where thousands of people attended and met God. Everything was working for him, yet his heart began to falter. He did not stumble publicly but began to question and ponder God. He had a reputation of sound judgment, loving demeanor, and public influence, yet something changed. Characteristics of people in this stage tend to include confusion and reflection.

There is an ongoing argument with oneself. It feels as though you have everything. You have achieved and are influential. Yet, there is a sense of confusion as to why. Hagberg describes this time as a "time of gray." The past achievements seem so clear, yet the future seems terribly unknown. It is my contention that often at this stage, we will dismiss these feelings as a mid-life crisis (depending upon the age that you enter this stage).

I did. I immediately felt like I must be questioning out of boredom and needing something new in my life in which to achieve. It is at this stage we contemplate "being" rather than "doing." For many, this is frightening. We struggle to understand our mental health and our questions. How could I doubt God? What is wrong with me? Am I one of the "back sliders?" Am I apostate? The questions get more dramatic as we go along. Strangely, we never seem to question all we have believed until now, and then all the questions overwhelm us. I felt buried in my questions and simultaneously misunderstood for asking them. The shadows can get long in this stage. We strike back by pretending that all is okay, going through the motions so as to not rock the boat. We double down on our commitment to God. If we just read the Bible enough, or pray enough, or serve enough, we can get past this. How many of you can identify with me here?

I was a walking nightmare of contradiction. I served in so many different capacities within my previous church that I was often exhausted, yet I never said no. I thought the more engaged I was, the less time I would have for these seemingly intrusive thoughts. Then I would go home, but the questions would not stop. How can a loving God create a place like hell, let alone sentence millions of people there for eternity and then still call himself the savior of mankind? Why must I forgive my enemies and pray for those that persecute me, but

God has no such mandate? What possible reason could there be for someone's genitals to decide their talents and giftings in Christianity?

Interestingly, these are some of the tamer questions I quietly pondered. And, of course, in my public, I continued sticking to the script, saying all the right things. I smiled until my face hurt and then smiled harder. The devil was not getting me, no, sir!

Between stages four and five exists a somewhat precarious deterrent ... the wall! So, what is this wall? Well, it varies for each individual. Let me try to explain. Some time ago, my daughter convinced me to try a Spartan race. If you are familiar, you know the absolute punishment that you put your body through to complete the task. Depending upon which level race you run, you will see between 20 and 50 obstacles along with muddy and wet conditions. The distance differs at each level as well. I am deeply competitive, and I like to push myself, so I agreed. I was unprepared for the first race I ran. I could not run the entire race (okay, the majority of it). Numerous obstacles were difficult, and a few were unattainable. They ranged in degrees of difficulty so some seemed to come easy yet there were those few that just kicked my ass.

One of the more seemingly easy obstacles is an A-frame cargo net climb. I would imagine that most people upon arriving at this obstacle are happy for somewhat of a break. That would not be me. I approached that "wall" and started up. About halfway up, I was confronted with my fear of heights (not to mention my exhaustion) and I froze. I could not move and started to panic. Those climbing at my rear had to deviate around me. My daughter was also behind me, and I begged her to go ahead so I could see her. Nothing was working! Sitting on top of the A-frame was a woman I did not know. Recognizing my panic, she yelled down to me to get my attention. As

I looked at her, she asked me to focus on her and to go one rung at a time. She yelled, she encouraged, and she did not stop until I made it to the top. Swinging your body over the top to the other side is another confrontation altogether. It took me a while, but I managed to slowly climb down the other side. I mentally struggled with that near failure, asking myself over and over what was wrong with me. I berated myself, knowing I was stronger than that, but finally I had to just admit that the wall was terrifying *for me*.

As Hagberg describes in her book, "the wall" is not an actual physical wall, but a wall of ego. Stage five is the point of our journey where we must examine our own ego. It is here that all those shadow traits make their appearance known to us, and we must decide if we want to push through. Think for a moment of all your failings. Look back into your past and examine your present. You will find things about yourself that you struggle with and do not want others to know. I am reminded of the scene in Star Wars in which Luke Skywalker, while training with Yoda, feels a pull to enter the Dagobah cave. Here, Luke believes he has met up with Darth Vadar only to realize (after awesomely saber slicing Vadar's head off) that it is Luke's head in the infamous black helmet. Daunting, indeed! Yet, there is transformation waiting for us on the other side (though not necessarily the dark side), and it beckons us onward at our own pace. While we all experience this wall differently, there are common traits.

We all feel comfortable with what we know. It is only when we are confronted with conflicting information that we react, and it is usually a negative reaction. I know very few who when confronted with information that challenges their paradigm who will fist pump and shout, "Oh Yeah!" At the wall, all we think we know comes into question, and there is a desire to let go of certainty and intellect. You might call this faith, but, personally, it just feels like defeat to me.

Some experience physical symptoms, others deal with emotional problems. It is a battle to let go of the ego as it does not go quietly into that good night.

Along with this deficit in intellect is the need to relinquish control. I am a huge control freak, so this was just an absolute no for me for a long time. In the last year, I have had to come to conclusion that I am unable to control others and their behaviors. While I may care and have deep feelings for them, it is in no way my responsibility to make their choices or control their behavior, even if I am better at it!

My very good friend Jamal Jivangee has discussed with me and quite a few others the idea of the shadow-self. I do not necessarily remember him using those words, yet, in our discussions, he often asked me to evaluate what others are mirroring back to me. Confronting our shadow-self is often difficult because we do not recognize its traits. Recently, Jamal had me consider the people in my life who generate some sort of negative emotional response in me. The idea is in doing so I will begin to recognize myself in them. It is projection at its finest. I detest or dislike things about others yet fail to recognize my guilt in the same attributes. In all honesty, every time we have a discussion surrounding that, it pisses me off. I stay angry about it for a while, but when I return and reevaluate, I find that it is accurate.

At this point, you might think that the goal is to distance yourself from your shadow qualities, but, actually, that is the opposite. We must learn to embrace this side of ourselves. No, no, that does not mean you get to be an ass and revel in them. Instead each time they arise, ask what is being learned from them. When we stop hiding from ourselves, justifying our behavior, and get serious about discovering all that we are, we will find our core, or our soul. This is where healing occurs!

So, what happens if we avoid the wall? I mean, after all, we are not required to attempt the climb. Hagberg elaborates on this idea. Her contention is that we will have one of two outcomes: either we will find ourselves perpetually in a dark place or we will retreat to an earlier stage. As it pertains to the subject of deconstruction, I believe this to be the place where many lose their faith for a time. They cannot go back, yet they cannot go forward and so chose instead to sit in the dark. This will work temporarily, but, eventually, we all need light.

This is exactly where I have found myself in the last year. I wanted to shut off everything associated with God. No theological study, no discussions. I simply sat in my despair and anger as though the dark was my new reality. Often, we spiritualize this, referring to it as our desert as though we are traveling as the Israelites did. I have even heard others comment that they have learned to become nomads. I have an appreciation for this line of thinking but am unable to be satisfied with it. I find myself reflecting at this point. I missed having a relationship with God. Not the god that I grew up being told about, but the idea of who God should truly be. This point led others to accuse me of making God in my own image, yet I cannot get past the idea that God should be grace and mercy and love and acceptance. I really want nothing to do with a god that I must constantly appease in order to have a relationship. I always feel bad saying so, but this type of god reminds me of a three-year-old child stomping his foot and demanding his way.

That did not go over well in my house with my kids, so why would I want a god that does the same? I have spent my time working on me and examining my shadow-self, and now I am seeking purpose and wisdom. Ironically, moving into stage five means that anyone not yet in this stage will notice a change in us just in time to coincide with our inability to care what others think. We are emerging into the light!

Here is where it gets a bit confusing for me. The reason it does so is simply because I do not have much experience, if any, at these last two stages. Stage five is power by purpose. I remember hearing about living from purpose while in the church, but usually someone else was deciding my purpose or challenging me with personality tests and classes to decide in which area of ministry I belonged. This is a unique stage in that it relies on each person's inner strength. It is here we become much more familiar and comfortable with our own inner dialogue and voice. We trust ourselves and our instincts. This stage requires courage. You put yourself out there and live from the values that you define as valuable. I identified these recently as love, peace, joy, mercy, and empathy. Through the lens of these values that I evaluate my life and those in it. It much easier now to forgive those that have hurt me because my values dictate the way in which I choose to approach them.

Achievements no longer have as much meaning. You are much more apt to pass on your wisdom and find encouragement in others achieving than to selfishly guard your own ideas. As it pertains to the deconstructive process, I have found that I am no longer worried about where I am in this compared to where others are in their own processes. I am comfortable in my journey (well, not always comfortable, but I am not worried that my journey should look like someone else's). So, what do people in this stage look like? They are often accepting of themselves. They appear courageous and calm. There is a sense of contentment for where they are on their path. They no longer demand of themselves that they grow or improve. They realize they already are doing both. Often spirituality will once again come to the forefront. No longer involved in religious requirements, they are free to explore their spirituality and God. I know, I know, it sounds all new age, but this is where peace resides.

One of my favorite descriptions of people at this stage is that of discerning. "Discerning" is a word often used in Christian circles to denote those individuals that are capable of hearing the difference between voices or spirits, or ourselves and God. If I had a prophetic word to share in church, I would struggle with myself as to whether it was really God or just me wanting to say something. It would often come down to feeling as though I needed to vomit in order to speak the words. I am learning however to differentiate my voice from God's. I think we all hear from God, but many of us doubt it and never learn the value of divine communication.

Now, of course, just because we have faced our wall does not mean we avoid the shadow side, but the shadows are smaller. There is a temptation to ignore the existence of our own shadow side. We can get comfortable and forget there is still work do on ourselves as well as lessons to be learned. Stage five people are often thought of as impractical by those that are motivated by achievement. This stage is a slower more introspective stage. More thought goes into our decisions and actions.

There is a stage 6 (consisting of wisdom), but I will not spend much time there because I have no idea what it looks like and can only describe what I have read. I have no anecdotal, spiritual examples here. I can only say that this stage looks like sacrifice. In some way, this stage brings an individual full circle. Once again there is a sense of powerlessness, but it is such that it comes from a place of peace not striving for more. One can sit in silence and be content even to the point of death. There is a resolution of life and understanding. If any shadow exists here it is only the appearance of not fearing danger. I think of Jesus here. While he was horribly tortured and suffered physically, he was able to ask for the forgiveness of those harming him.

There was no fear of death, only commitment to the cause of showing that God looked different than what humanity has surmised.

I am sure you can pick out examples of each of these stages from your own experience. Remember no one moves from one stage to the next without re-examining an earlier stage every now and then. No rhyme or reason, just living.

RELATIONSHIPS

The beginning of wisdom is to call things by their right names, or something like that. The process we are discussing has been called a lot of different things. Everyone seems to have their own term to apply to this deeply painful and introspective journey. Here are a few that I have heard and used: deconstruction, destruction, journey, process, crisis of faith, metamorphosis. The list goes on. So, are we talking about the same thing? Well, I am not sure that we can ever be specifically talking about the same thing. We each experience it differently and, for a time, each of those names may apply.

I have referred to this process in my life as deconstruction and for a time, I believed that it only had to do with my religious beliefs. However, I found this is more of a metamorphosis. There is a change, but that has been *my* experience. Maybe, for you, it is just a change or question of religious belief. One is no greater than the other; they are all a choice to introspectively examine us.

Ironically, I have witnessed people's arguments as to how we should refer to the experience. Not too long ago, a well-known pastor came out with a blog addressing this situation. He likened the process of examining our belief structure to that of restoring a piece of art. It was a beautiful description of loving care surrounding our ideas of

God. Strangely, I found myself somewhat insulted by his take that those expressing anger, bitterness, and disappointment were cheating themselves (my interpretation). I got angrier. Now, as I examine that response, I understand a little better. While that may have been *his* experience, it is *not* everyone's experience. Subjectivity rules the day! We each have a perspective that is dependent upon our background, family, culture, belief structure, personality, and the circumstances that bring us to this place.

A while back I was involved in a conversation about just this subject. You see there is a very real definition of deconstruction that has nothing to do with religious beliefs. It is more about the unity of text, using the right words, and agreeing on definitions. As such, one of the people involved in the conversation shared a small snippet of his journey. I have included it because I feel it mirrors quite a few people's confusion and emotion surrounding these ideas.

"What I had was a crisis of faith, it was completely unintentional. I found out about history and theology and my faith pretty much fell apart. It has taken a long time to get back to really experiencing and believing in God. My faith made it through a terrible, painful, and spiteful attack. It was not a knowledgeable, intentional, or systematic examination of my beliefs. It was 'Oh crap, that's not true...and that and that and that. I guess none of it is.' I don't encourage my experience on anyone and have become far less rigid about what others believe compared to what I believe. I've learned love, grace, and mercy through my faith crisis. I see deconstruction as intentional and purposeful. It was not meant to destroy one's faith. What I went through was destructive, I did not deconstruct."

SHAD

My response to this conclusion:

"I've come to see the experience as a psychological impact. So much of what we are taught in conservative evangelical Christianity is structured around identity that in this experience, we lose ourselves for a while. It is a crisis of faith and to some extent, a crisis of self, but I think eventually (if we survive that), it becomes the traditional understanding of deconstruction. It does begin to shift and rebuild on a continuous basis once we are past the psychological trauma."

In this short exchange, we identified very different experiences even though they may have certain markers in common. That will always be the case. We will each bring to the table those things that are specific to our experience.

REACTIONS AND RESPONSES

An individual's subjective experience as well as personality is the reason we see a multitude of responses to the process of deconstruction. There are no right or wrong reactions. Some are angry, some elated. Some are sad, confused, and the list goes on as many emotions as you can imagine. For many, just sitting in a church building triggers an emotional response that sometimes may not be understood. It is that way for me. I can no longer go to a church service. I literally find my lip curling upwards. That is not to say that I have a problem if others attend church, I just do not desire to myself.

So, what kind of reactions did you get when you began to process and ask questions? As I have already explained, those with whom I attended church were less than appreciative of my questioning, and I have not heard from any of them since leaving the building. That surprised me, but I do understand the psychological implications of maintaining a relationship with someone who is questioning your closely held beliefs. It is destabilizing. For a short while afterward, I shut down emotionally. Sunday morning would come, and I would feel a sense of guilt for not being inside the building serving in some capacity. In order to deal with the emotional fallout, I started hiking those mornings just so I could feel close to God through nature. It was amazingly restorative and along the way, I reconnected with some friends that shared the experience. We even jokingly began to call our weekly hikes "church." It was during those times that I expressed my anger and sadness. I pulled no punches with language and attitude. Surprisingly, it was met with acceptance and even admiration that I, as a Christian, could be so open about my disappointments with God, church, and friends. It opened dialogue that surrounded the subject of God and religion with someone who would not have discussed it with anyone else. I was able to share my thoughts on how God should be if He is love. Those discussions were healing and cathartic. I treasure them still even though we no longer hike together as often.

KAFKA AND THE BEETLE

What about those that seem to now espouse some sort of atheistic belief system or at the very least agnostic? I want to share an old story by Kafka about a beetle found in his work, *Metamorphosis*. I will briefly explain the story, and I think you will see the correlation. The basic premise is quite bizarre. The main character, Gregor wakes to find himself turning into a beetle. What is truly interesting is not Gregor's transformation, but the reactions of those around him. First there is concern for his well-being as he is late getting up and leaving for work. His mother and sister, concerned, come to his door to encourage him to arise and get ready. Gregor tries to respond, but his voice has changed, and the women they are having difficulty understanding him. Shortly thereafter, his boss arrives and, along with his father, threaten Gregor. Finally, he answers the door, but all are shocked at his appearance and distance themselves from him. As time goes on, Gregor becomes more comfortable with his new appearance, but those around him are no longer comfortable making concessions for him in their lives. They become angry, separating themselves from this new Gregor. Any time that Gregor is around his family or friends, there is a distinct apprehension. Gregor quickly realizes he must isolate himself. Sadly, Gregor dies and those that were family and friends feel a sense of relief that they are no longer required to interact and quickly go on with their lives.

Now, please hear me out. I am not suggesting that those identifying as agnostic or atheistic are somehow a gross bug. Instead, the family's response represents the catalyst for an agnostic mindset as some travel through this deconstruction process. When we begin to ask questions, those within our belief structure find themselves somewhat uncomfortable. At first, they encourage us in our faith and suggest ways in which we can fight against what they presume to be demonic influence (at least in my experience).

Eventually, however, there is social distancing as smiles slowly turn to plastic. It is a façade! They no longer understand us in our new transformative appearance nor the language that we now speak. It finally becomes a situation in which we have little in common but understand that a change is necessary. Often this change is separation. Just as Gregor finally succumbs to death (not made clear as to whether is a natural death or one by suicide), those leaving the institutional church wander in somewhat darkness. For some, this darkness becomes the new normal or, at the very least, a temporary sanctum as they work through the harsh reactions of those that are supposed to be the bearers of light.

I am probably not making the connection very well for you, and it sounds as though I am seeing atheism and agnosticism as negatives. Please hear my heart, I am not. This is just the best way I can explain the process as I see it and as I experience it. I am currently living with the fact that I am quite agnostic most days. Some days I question whether I have moved into full blown atheism. For some who identify as atheist, this is a peaceful place and they are quite happy there. That is why I hesitate with my example because I certainly am not maligning their choice. However, it is often there that those of their former lives point to and claim that the person is apostate, thereby, creating even more hurt feelings and damaged emotions.

It is probably prudent here to discern between an agnostic and an atheist. Can't we do both? Well yes, actually, we can. An agnostic just believes that knowing if there is a god(s) is impossible. They have no form or idea of what this God looks like. An atheist has no belief of a deity at all. You can encompass both beliefs and adopt the term agnostic atheist. It gets confusing, at least for me. Many who wander in this desert of discontent with the current system often find themselves in one of these two camps. In my experience with others, it is far more prevalent to become agnostic, and in all honesty, this is where I find myself. As someone who was raised in the Christian belief system, this is somewhat of a shocking place to find myself. As a matter of fact, early in this process, it was suggested to me that I might find myself exactly where I am. I could not believe that would be the case.

It is my contention that many find themselves here because the God they have always known is now subject to scrutiny and he is just not living up to the hype of a loving God. I mean just read the Old

Testament and you will find a god that is no better than many of his contemporaries. Many books have been written on this subject, yet a majority of Christians will still excuse away seemingly bad behavior by God just because he is God. Just mention that God is supposed to be synonymous with love and you will hear immediate arguments that suggest he is also just. Mention mercy, and you will find those that suggest God cannot be in the presence of sin. Go ahead, let's do another challenge. Go to your social media page and just type the words "God is love and that is all he is." Watch what happens!

Now try to reconcile God with Jesus who is supposed to be the personification of God, and you will have a real problem on your hands. They do not match! Well, Jesus does not match our traditional understanding of God. So, did God actually go through this changing process as well or do we just have God all wrong? Or have you asked yourself, as I have, if God even exists? This is where a lot of the reactions you get start getting angry.

REACTIONS

The fallout of deconstructing a belief system is more than just stumbling through the darkness and trying to understand what you believe. There are very real effects that rumble through our lives. Most have experienced some interruption in the relationships in their lives. We have discussed the reaction of those that now view you as different within our church communities but what about your very own family and close friends? There is often a large amount of upheaval in these relationships as well. No one is in the exact same place within this process, so the chances of those around you understanding where you stand are slim, especially if they have not yet started the questioning process. You are suddenly suspect.

I will share with you a deeply painful time in my own life. My husband was raised in the church as well. He has a lot of the same foundational beliefs that I did. We both drifted away from the church for a while in our younger years and had come back, as often happens, because we had a family. Most want their children raised in their belief system, so it is not surprising to find yourself back in a pew with a few children. We generally find a church in which we feel comfortable, one that is preaching and teaching those tenets with which we are familiar. So, when one of the two in a marriage begins to question, this leads to some discomfort. Both my husband and I became increasingly uncomfortable, but it was only me that had starting to change my perspective. After the drama of separating from the church, I was carrying a lot of guilt and blamed myself for my whole family losing their place in the church community. I knew that my questions were a large part of the issues, and while there were other problems, it was that issue that I kept coming back to.

The questions continued and so, from time to time, I would mention aloud something that I was pondering. I remember vividly the evening I mentioned that I was not sure I believed the Bible anymore. I mean there is a lot of useful information there, but I was struggling with inerrancy. My husband became very agitated and started yelling at me. He was standing over me as I was sat on the couch. I just remember sitting there crying while he yelled that he did not know who I was anymore. It was devastating. For quite some time, I wondered if this journey was going to result in a broken family. There were lots of other altercations surrounding beliefs, and his struggle to understand my struggles.

Around the same time, one of my daughters was becoming more serious in her romantic relationship and was discussing marriage. As such, my husband and I met her potential in-laws and spent some time getting to know one another. As is common in these types of discussions, we were asked where we went to church. Because of all that had occurred, we were without a church home. My husband attended here and there, but I had no desire to go. As such, I said so. Several weeks later, my daughter came to me and wanted to chat. She had a question as to whether I thought people should attend church. I responded that everyone should decide for themselves. She was visibly upset, so I asked why she wanted to know. It turned out that she had been speaking with her future mother-in-law who was very concerned that I did not attend church. I have to say, it angered me, but I tried to hold onto my demeanor. I responded that it was not her place to defend me since she was unsure of where I was (as was I), and if her mother-in-law had questions, she could come directly to me.

I remember once again feeling so responsible for the angst in my family's lives. Further, I was watching my other daughter struggle more and more emotionally from the fall out of our church separation. There are other examples of relationship problems I endured during this process, but I am sure you get the idea. I am not alone in this. I have heard heartbreaking stories of families falling apart, generations of families not speaking to one another, and the always sacrosanct sounding words of "I will pray for you" by those that have seemingly little interest in what you are experiencing. While I do not know this for sure, I feel pretty confident that those prayers are that I will pull my head out of my ass and go back to believing the way they believe, but that is just a guess.

GOD AS A WEAPON

S o, we have all been there or observed someone else's misfortune as it pertains to the "fear of God." No, I do not mean the fear of God that is often referenced with regard to awe or reverence. I am specifically speaking about those instances in which God is referenced as a threat. You know the shtick … God will smite you for some incorrect belief or action. Hell is waiting for you if you step out of line. God is sitting around with a clipboard keeping score … . wait … love keeps no record of wrongs, right? Not in my experience, and I am positive not in the experience of many others.

RELIGION IS A MASK

Religion is just a mask! The reality is that we put on different mask each day in order to deal with our circumstances. We all like to think that we are authentically us all the time but if we are honest, it just is not true. We adapt to circumstances. I mean think about how many times you have politely smiled and held in a comment that you were thinking. Church and religious relationships are no different. In fact, I think the religious environment creates many situations in which we feel it necessary to behave other than we might want to behave. The standing joke often heard refers to the absolute chaos and bickering that occurs in households while getting ready to go to church only to arrive and pretend that all is just perfect. And we are oh so spiritual. It is fodder for comedians, but it is also very true, or at least it was in my house.

Life is messy, yet we feel obligated to put on a happy face because, after all, we are #blessed. But what happens when all the fake happiness and pretend spirituality does not cut it in real life situations? What happens when the mask comes off and you just let people see the shit show that is your life? Few and far between are those that will stand next to you. Most will back away, not because they are bad people or even uninterested, but more so because they themselves have no idea how to respond. I can respect that as long as it is honestly communicated.

I remember vividly one of the few times that I opened up to someone about the pain I was feeling. There was a look of stunned surprise, and then the woman said, "I do not think I can help you; you are just too needy and hurt." Devastating. But I will say that looking back that I can find respect for her bluntness. In the moment I felt so rejected, stupid, and ashamed, and quite honestly, I cannot imagine saying those words to anyone, especially when they are in pain, but at least she was honest. The lesser honest response is that polite, plastic smile as the person backs away slowly. Or, even worse, they go on the offensive.

Anyone who has questioned a religious belief, or a political belief, or just a regular belief knows that someone is bound to disagree. If only it stopped at disagreement. I am still often amazed at the ugly vitriolic junk that people say to one another because of disagreement over an idea or belief. I personally believe it goes back to the protection of oneself and the brain and conscious processes taking place. We must push back. We must argue our point. This is a very real part of the process of deconstruction. Once I started questioning, I found myself often intimidated in conversations because it was oh so easy to realize that I knew nothing. Thinking back that is exactly where I needed to be ... knowing nothing and being uncertain. Why? Because I am less inclined to argue vehemently and hurt others when I am in a place of humbleness as it pertains to what I know. Alas, that is not the reality for a period of time. When we begin to explore, question, read, and learn, we find space for confidence. We are suddenly confronted with new information, and it leads to a place of certainty again.

Somewhere within this newfound confidence resides a debate. Scroll through your social media feeds and you will notice all the arguing. I was one of them. When I started better understanding religious concepts that I had never been aware of, I instantly had an opinion. I exercised that opinion on the regular. I will confess that from time to time, I still get a little heated and will jump into a conversation to explain why everyone else has no idea what they are talking about, but those moments are much rarer now.

THE NEED TO CORRECT AND RIDICULE

One thing, however, that I have never understood is the need to ridicule someone else for where they are in the process. I recognized early on that we are all on different journeys having started from different places. As such, ridiculing someone for a belief that you no longer hold seems somewhat misplaced. After all, at some point you were no better. Typically, the only time I engage now is when someone is treating another person badly with name calling or vitriolic sarcasm. I know it's tough to believe that I can be sarcastic, but trust me, I am adept.

The need to ridicule others masks a lack of self-confidence. Pointing out the flaws in others allows us to feel superior or at the very least, shift the attention from ourselves. It's petty, but so much a part of this process, first as a defense mechanism as someone who is unhappy that someone is questioning our neat little belief system and then later on, as a way in which to deal with the faltering emotions that this process seems to bring out. This leads to a desire to correct. My least favorite word from someone else is "actually ... " This usually means they are about to point out all the ways in which my perspective falls short.

So, let's talk about two differing ideas that seem somewhat related—clarity and correctness. Clarity is being sure about what we believe. It is clear and concise in our minds and, therefore, is not to be questioned, at least by a well-reasoned person. Correctness relates to clarity in that it is a belief that our beliefs are correct in a cultural or moral context. Depending upon our reasoning, we are more apt to be cooperative or competitive. A paper featured in the July 2014 issue of Personality and Social Psychology Bulletin, "Attitude Certainty and Conflict Style," the authors suggest the more strongly an individual believes their attitude is correct, the more competitive they will be in any discussion surrounding the subject matter. So, let's put this in context to our discussion.

If I am involved in a discussion surrounding a religious belief, and I feel that I am correct in my assertions as well as in my attitude, I am more apt to become competitive in my conversation and feel a need to convince others to agree with me. We have all experienced this. Everyone has a Thanksgiving Day story. We all have a relative that is opinionated, loud, and positive they are correct regardless of the conversation subject. They feel a need to convince you that their political stance or religious experience is valid and should be the correct perspective. Social media enhances this experience in that we are not face-to-face with those involved in conversations. Keyboard warriors abound and are usually very adept at presenting their argument, explaining why you are wrong. In the eventuality that they cannot convince you, they usually offer a parting shot at your parentage, obvious upcoming trip to hell, or your associations, right before they block you and feel self-righteous in doing so because they do not need the negativity in their lives. Yes, I am being sarcastic!

Somewhere in all those conversations is the assumptions that God is on our side. Our beliefs line up exactly with how God intended the universe to work and as such, the creator endorses our statements. This mindset drives me crazy. In the recent past, I have quit arguing because it does no good. I can usually be found either not engaging any longer in the conversation or giving the other person what they desire, the win! My good friends who are Girardian in their thinking know that one of the quickest ways to de-escalate an argument is to capitulate. Give up the item that the other so desires, and the competition goes away. It is hurtful, however, to be targeted when God is the weapon.

Within the deconstruction process, we are already so inclined to find fault with our own thinking and reasoning, and as such, if you are me, every time someone accuses you of being wrong, your first inclination is to believe it. Maybe God really is angry at me as I have always believed. Maybe God is just waiting around the corner to smite me. Maybe I alone am the only one who has no idea about the character of God. Wait a minute, nope, cannot believe that to be true.

God is a convenient threat for those that need to be right. After all, he is not actually involved in the conversation, so we are free to speak in his name all we want. Except that many believe God *is* involved in the conversation. We have the word of God, the Bible, the Canon, and our favorite translation to make our cherry-picked argument for us. Using the Bible to beat someone up is cowardly in my opinion, yet it still seems to be one of the most well-used ways in which to influence someone.

Following closely behind is the need that some have to blame individuals, groups, or even whole countries for elemental and weather issues. Every time there is some devastating natural disaster, you can count on the articles, blogs, and social media posts of those weaponizing God. (Sidebar: Is it just me or does God spend an inordinate amount of time focusing on the United States and our wayward ways in which to make his points?)

Regardless of how people grossly misinterpret God, why is it so effective? The reason itself is simple—it plays on our base fears. It is the existential fear of death and what comes after that often is the catalyst for a relationship with God, so it makes sense that this fear continues to be effective in manipulating our senses and behaviors. Complicating things further are phobias. A phobia is a strong, persistent, and unwarranted fear of either a situation or an object. There are an amazing number of phobias and even one in which someone can be afraid of phobias (Phobophobia, no I am not kidding). The fear of the Lord or God (not the biblical kind) is called theophobia. You can literally be afraid of God to the point of panic attacks and nightmares. Along the same lines is that of atheophobia, which is the fear of not having God in your life. See, damned if you do and damned if you don't. Sorry bad joke!

It becomes easy to see why those barbs thrown at us from friends, family, or even strangers on the internet are so hurtful. They play into some base fear that we have even if it has not reached the proportion of an actual phobia. Even laughing off some of the comments thrown my way has still produced subconscious thoughts of being on God's bad side. One "gentleman" in a conversation once told me to let him know "what sulfur smelled like." This was his oh so Christian way of telling me he thought I was going to hell, all for asking a question. There is that Christian love! That was my response, but seriously, somewhere within my subconscious, that fear remains. My final word on this subject is this ... if you are going to throw shade at someone for questions or believing differently than you do, please do us all a favor and act like it hurts you that someone may be going to hell. If you are going to use God as a weapon, please do so sparingly and with great remorse.

LABELING THEORY

We have all heard the name calling that seems to accompany any type of reflection pertaining to religious beliefs. Step outside the denominational box and someone will be waiting to label you. Ironically, these labels almost always seem to be negative, or what we deem negative anyway. I believe this is one of the biggest stumbling blocks to the process. No one wants to be outside the group. After all, there is power and protection in the group. My mimetic theory friends would see in this inclination the beginnings of a mob and scapegoating, but I digress. I have been called many things over the last five or six years. It starts out with gentle cautioning and concern with where you may be headed in your questioning. As soon as it gets uncomfortable for others, however, there is a subtle distancing that then becomes more obvious, and then the labeling starts.

So, let's talk about labeling. I find myself often denouncing the use of labels, but, honestly, we all use them. Democrat, Republican, conservative, liberal, Protestant, Catholic, heretic, fundamental, etc. I am sure you already have several others running through your mind just reading those few. My problem with labels is that I feel they allow us to dismiss one another. Let me explain.

Early in my process of evaluating my beliefs, I came across the subject of universal salvation. Hold on, stay with me, I know this subject leads to stress for a lot of people, but it is just an example. Universalism is not an easy subject although it is often made to sound that way. First and foremost, there are several different beliefs that seem to fall under this one term (kind of like all the terms for hell in the Bible). Radical universalism which claims only one God, but he is accessible through all religions. Liberal universalism claims that as Christ redeemed mankind through incarnation, that all will be saved eventually. Evangelical universalism contends that even those unevangelized will be saved. There is even a belief in biblical universalism which states that the term universal is indicative only of all nations and tongues being represented in salvation. There are others as well. My head hurts, does yours? Regardless, the actual arguments around universalism are not my point. You are free to explore this discussion on your own. I am interested only in so far as it pertains to the response to the word.

I dare you to suggest on your social media platform that you are considering universalism. Go ahead, I will wait, it will not take long. The majority of responses will not include any questions as to what type of universalism you are talking about or why you are drawn to such questions. Rather, the responses will be wholesale agreement or wholesale disagreement. Those disagreeing will most often include dire warnings of leading people astray or hell itself as a result of asking questions. It is a fascinating process! So why won't people ask you questions? Because they already have an idea of the definition of the word in their head. That pesky naïve realism kicks in and their perception is reality and objective truth. I hope you hear the sarcasm coming through here. If they disagree with the definition they understand of the label, just hearing you mention it will trigger their response. They no longer are interested in what you think or the questions you have as in their mind, you are already labeled and as such, dismissed. See what I mean?

So, there is an actual theory surrounding this idea, I did not just pull it out of thin air. Labeling theory in sociological terms is used to describe the process of people coming to identify and behave in ways that align with labels others have used to describe them. It is most often used in context to criminal behavior. If we label and treat someone as a criminal or a deviant person, eventually, they will come to act in such a manner. Consider the same phenomenon in education. If a teacher labels a student as a problem student or stupid, the child will begin to exhibit the behavior or intelligence level that is expected.

This can work positively as well. I remember when I was raising my children. I spent a lot of time pointing out their positive attributes and their potential for success. I have heard it said that people rise to the level of expectation that others put on them. If the level assigned to you is low (or socially unacceptable), you will perform as such.

Now let's apply this to religious belief and expectations of religious expression. If someone expresses an interest in universalism as was the previous example, those hearing it and applying their own understanding to the term, will begin to label and treat you as they view the term, often negatively. The word "heretic" gets tossed around a lot and has been the subject of several books, one by a very good friend of mine. In his book *Heretic!* Matthew Distefano outlines quite a few issues that come up with regard to Christian beliefs and the questions surrounding those beliefs. For doing so, he has received quite a few nasty comments that question his intelligence and salvation. In what I believe to marketing genius, he used several of the horrible responses he received as quotes on the book as though they were positive comments. I will share one of those comments with you because I believe it illustrates what I am saying. "I know it's hard, but actually reading the Bible can really illuminate what God actually thinks on topics. Distefano is either a severely ignorant believer or a false teacher." Another equates him to "one with the devil." All this for questions and a different opinion.

Those who are so often considered and labeled a heretic will finally give up and embrace the terminology. I have; I no longer care what names people ascribe to me and if I am honest, there is almost a sense of reveling in the label. In other words, if that is what they think of me, then I should go out of my way to ensure it is true. It is a rebellion against the system.

The above, however, outlines "the halo effect." In a nutshell, this idea centers around cognitive bias. My overall impression of a person will impact my evaluation of characteristics about that person. If I find the person "nice," there is a tendency to then believe all good things about their character such as they are smart or generous. I may have no evidence of either, but per my experience that I found them to be nice (again subjective and subject to experience), I will believe other characteristics that I deem to go along with nice. This works in the opposite, as well. If I believe someone to fit my definition of a heretic, I am more apt to believe they possess other "negative" traits as well. As the writer of the review above shows, he feels Matthew is ignorant, a false teacher, and even in league with the devil. Each of those beliefs about Matthew are a direct result of labeling and the halo effect. Now regardless of the subject matter, this reader will never find agreement with Matthew (outside of extraordinary circumstances) because he has summarily dismissed him. I find this to be very dehumanizing. We diminish people to ideas rather than seeing them as loved by God. When done as believers, I find this to be at odds with the overall ideas of Christianity.

SHAME AND TRAUMA

I cannot remember a time when I was without shame. It seems like it is embedded within me so deeply that it is fundamental to my being. Sad right? I am not even completely sure where it comes from, but I have some ideas. I am going to share something very personal and deeply painful. It is going to make some uncomfortable, but that is not my goal. My goal is a deep conversation about shame and the absolute devastation that it brings with it to someone's life, and how it is exacerbated by religious thought and tradition.

As a child and into my early teens, I was repeatedly sexually assaulted. The main perpetrator was someone I knew very well. It was a constant. I was afraid to go to sleep at night, afraid to be in the house alone with this person, afraid to tell anyone. Why? Several reasons come to mind. First and foremost, this person was wildly violent, and you never knew what was going to be the impetus for a reaction. I was afraid of what he would do to those I loved if they confronted him.

Second, I was not honestly sure anyone would believe me. So, I shut myself inside myself and just functioned. I lived up to my responsibilities and the expectations of others and kept my mouth shut. So, what does this have to do with religious deconstruction or a deep life transformation? It was the beginning of shame, I think, and something that has affected my entire life. Even just writing this small amount of introduction to the subject has my throat tight, tears in my eyes, and a slightly queasy feeling in my stomach. I am 55 years old and still feel the emotions of that little girl. I have had to take several deep breaths and remind myself that it is okay to talk about this subject when all I want to do in once again close in on myself and pretend none of it was real.

I grew up in church. I was raised to believe that sex was for marriage and having children. So, the sexual issues that were a part of my experience were confusing. Many have heard and read about the purity movement. When I was younger, I did not know it had a name, it was just what I was taught. God loved pure girls. I am sure he loved pure boys too, but not having that experience, I could not identify with it. So, here was my conundrum: if God valued purity and virginity until marriage, how could I ever find favor with God? I was damaged goods. Little girls who grow up having had sexual assault as a part of their experience tend to be damaged physically, but also mentally and emotionally. No one tells you there is something wrong with you, you already know it. So, you start hiding yourself or doing things that will drive people away from you.

I remember when I was in the 7th grade. I actually decided that I would not wash my hair. It seemed like a defense mechanism to me although I did not have that understanding at the time, I just wanted to be left alone. I do not remember how long of a time I went but it was a least several weeks. Looking back, I see depressive symptoms there as well but mainly just a hope that I would be gross enough to be left alone. You see how shame begins to take hold.

Another coping mechanism is that of acting as though everything was okay. I just swallowed my emotion and went on with what I was supposed to be doing. I became an actress and a damn good one. No one knew what was happening and on some small scale, I felt better. At least no one knew my shame. As I got older and boys became a focus, I wanted so badly to have a boyfriend but struggled with the idea at the same time. I deeply wanted to feel loved and valued and most who have a history with sexual molestation will tell you that they seek it out inappropriately. There came a time when sex was something I used to get attention and what I hoped would be love.

Now looking back, I can see that this is wildly inappropriate and damaging in itself, but then I just was reacting. Some girls shut down sexually after abuse, others become promiscuous. I have done both, but promiscuity definitely came first. I do not mean to give the impression that it was a constant thing, but on some level even then, I knew I was still trying to be okay and normal. But I was keenly aware afterwards that God was not happy with me. I remember thinking often that I was already damaged goods so God could not be more pissed off at me than he already was. What difference did it make?

Now, let me jump ahead in time because I can get mired down in the remembrances of that time in my life for quite a while if I allow it. I chose to go into the military. I had been on my own for a while. I had graduated high school living without my family. I had completed some college but slacked off and was honestly making a mess of my life, so I decided to let someone else run the show for a while.

Looking back, it was difficult, but it allowed me to relax a bit. I know that sounds counter intuitive to what most consider military life to be, but when you grow up with sexual assault and violence, you tend to see life differently than most. I did not have to worry about paying rent. I did not have to worry about where my next meal was coming from. I just had to do as I was told. I was already a pro at that, so it was not a big deal to me. I slept when I was told to, ate when I was told to, and I lived where I was told to. I existed, but I was still missing that feeling of connection. I had walked away from God because I felt like that was a no-win situation as well. As a woman in the military, you are definitely in the minority, so it is not surprising to find yourself in a relationship. I met my husband at Camp Pendleton California in 1986. I still remember what he was wearing, and the first words he ever spoke to me. Looking back, I honestly still feel that rush of attraction and disbelief that he spoke to me. We have been married for 33 years, and occasionally, I still feel that sense of disbelief.

We were married after about a year and a half of a really difficult relationship. I came from a background replete with arguing and violence and that was my go-to in order to handle a situation. It did not help that for me, the tension of an argument did not go away until violence occurred, so I pushed hard at times to make that happen, just so I could relax. Yep, pretty warped! Regardless, we married and started our lives together. All good, right? Wrong! I was still walking around with a huge buildup of shame and self-disgust.

A married sex life does not function well in that environment. By then we had our first child and having children does something to you. It fundamentally changes your outlook on life. Hope seems to find its way back into your purview. At the very least, I wanted my child to know God even if I was permanently on the outside. So, I started going back to church. My husband was serving a tour in Japan at that time, so it was just me and my son. Going back to church seemed somewhat soothing and the repetition and system of it all made me feel better. I still had this very distrustful relationship with God but I was in his house every week so I thought maybe that would count for something.

Now here is where we get to the crux of the shame issue. I already walked around in a shame haze that had no foundation in religion yet, at the same time, seemed connected to God and my relationship with him. Now I have stepped back into an environment that seems to use shame and guilt as a motivator. I did not see it like that then but now it is obvious to me. For years, the purity movement had generated influence in the education system. Abstinence-based curriculums sprang up all over the country. Sex was reduced to procreation for most and created a whole generation of young men and women who were confused about sex, what constituted sex, and why it was considered immoral until some piece of paper was produced that said it was okay.

Those who indulged were stood in front of congregations to confess (yes that happened to a friend of mine). Note, *she* was forced to stand in front of the congregation and confess, not the boy involved. Unwed mothers and single parents were and sometimes still are, considered second-class congregants. I am sure you can think of many other situations or experiences that fall into this category. This does not even begin to include the numerous people suffering from addictions, diseases, and mental illness that are put into the same category—those on the outskirts of "normal." Shame inducing, indeed.

Brené Brown is a shame researcher. I am sure most of you have heard of her, read her books, or watched her amazing TED talk that started her public influence. In her book *I Thought It was Just Me*, she makes the statement that "shame is a silent epidemic." Her point is that we all experience shame. While she makes her point in all areas, I want to talk about shame in the church and how it affects us as we begin this process of deconstruction.

At the foundation of Christian belief is a doctrine called original sin. It is the belief that man is born sinful due to the sin of Adam and Eve in the garden of Eden. All of mankind is now under the curse of original sin. I never questioned this. The rhetoric already supported what I already felt about myself, so it made sense. We start at a negative value and can only hope to achieve ground zero. Several hundreds of years later, we have Jesus step onto the scene. The perfect, sinless lamb of God that takes away the sin of the world (or just those who believe it, depending upon your viewpoint). He is the cosmic good guy, the one who stands between us and an angry God. When we become aware of a relationship with God, we suddenly have all of these expectations of how to act, what to say, and how to look.

Some time back I wrote a piece on an experience of the altar that happens far too often in a lot of churches. We have all been there, either ourselves or watching it play out. The music is just right, the emotional atmosphere of the room is charged, people are praying or weeping, and suddenly someone steps forward and makes their way to the altar. Maybe an invitation was given or maybe it was just spontaneous need. Regardless, they slowly or purposely make their way to the front of the room and bow down on their knees seeking reconciliation with God. Beautiful right? I remember watching this play out one day in church. I should first remind you that I am empathic (I read the emotional atmosphere), and I have operated in the prophetic which has included visions.

As I watched this young woman approach the altar, I wept thinking how beautiful it was and identifying with the emotion that she was feeling. After some time and as she stood up to return to her seat, I was surprised to see a shadow fall into step beside her. At first, I was confused and looked around to see if anyone else was observing the same thing. It did not appear so, and I returned to watching the young woman. The shadow remained. As I continued to watch, it seemed to climb on her shoulders and begin to whisper in her ear. It was in this moment that I understood what I was seeing. It was shame, and it carried with it rules and expectations. She belonged now, was a part of the group, but along with that privilege came all the rules and expectation of following God. Dramatic, right?

Still gives me the creeps, but I understand it all too well, and I believe most experienced this in some form (not the vision, but the expectation and shame).

Shame is almost an expected identity in religion. It is celebrated to some extent as the impetus that leads us to Christ. Strangely, that is not the gospel (good news), but that is another subject altogether. We are often taught through Christianity that there is a mind-body split. Actually, I was taught that I was triune as was God. While God was father, son, and holy spirit, I was body, soul, and spirit. The spirit was considered the truly godly part of us. The body and soul were something that we endured until we died and received a heavenly body with which all would be right.

So, if you identify your body as something sinful that must be endured for a time, anything associated with bodily need or desire is considered "of the flesh" and must be controlled. Those that allow or participate in behaviors considered of the flesh are operating from a sinful nature. This is an open doorway to a lifetime of dealing with guilt and shame. There is a difference between guilt and shame. Guilt says I made a mistake; shame says I am a mistake. See the difference?

Let's examine for a moment one area of behavior that seems to strike a chord in the church: pornography. Most people have seen at least a small amount of what would be considered pornography. Of course, the definition is somewhat subjective, but for the sake of argument, let's use the example of an actual pornographic movie. Those living outside of a religious experience may struggle with what can be coined as a problem with pornography and even feel some concern about it, but it is not seen as a reflection of morals (unless we include cultural expectation).

Those within religion however struggle much more as there is not just a concern about morality, but they are often told it is a sickness or perversion that they must battle or even better, they are told they are dealing with demonic oppression. This produces shame, and the more someone identifies with what they are ashamed about, the greater propensity for the behavior to continue. I mentioned Brené Brown earlier. She has actual data that supports the idea that guilt is contra-indicated with "bad" behavior while shame is indicated in the continuation of the behavior. In other words, guilt works to keep us from poor behavior, but shame will bring us back to it every time. (Sidebar: I had a friend who used to identify himself as a sinner saved by grace.) Now most of us would agree with that label but it always bothered me. If I keep seeing myself as a sinner, what am I prone to do? Sin! If I live my life from an identity of shame about some behavior, what am I prone to do? Continue in the behavior that causes the shame. Now I am stuck in a feedback loop!

So, what happens when we begin to question our beliefs and maybe even God? What kind of reactions are we met with and how do those reactions affect us? For me, my initial questions were met with polite smiles and blank stares. The subject would be changed quickly, and my question dismissed as though I had not spoken. As I have shared elsewhere, the way in which I taught in the church began to change, and this produced short quips and sarcastic comments from those in the leadership of the church. The fascinating thing was that those I was teaching were making amazing progress with their relationships, addictions, and a varied amount of other issues.

My first questions pertained to the subject of grace so that is what I started including in my teaching. Shame does not allow for success though it may appear so for a while. You will be riding high on some new information, and it will quickly be followed by a reminder of what you perceive as your true identity. When I began to realize I was on the outside and that my questions were coming under scrutiny, I immediately felt as though I had done something wrong. My questions would not go away, my changing thoughts were still there but now they were accompanied by doubts and internal accusations. I spent quite a lot of time evaluating where I stood with God, wondering if I were one of those that was oppressed by the devil. Maybe all my new thoughts and questions were me being culled by Satan. After all, I was never sure I was in anyway.

Shame mimics trauma. Let's examine that for a moment. What is trauma? In short, trauma is a response to something deeply disturbing and overwhelms our physical body with feelings of not being able to cope, being helpless, and an inability to feel our emotions. Pretty dramatic right? We all handle trauma differently, but there are common markers psychologically. Many will feel emotionally, physically, and even cognitively overwhelmed.

While trauma can originate in a lot of places, when it begins in a religious experience, there is the added element of God being a part of the trauma. Even those that have expressed that they never were angry at God when they left the church eventually will have at least some small indicator of confusion as to how God can allow such things.

When the trauma is chronic, or long-lasting, there are added elements to the reaction. While there may be common markers in all trauma reactions, it really is a subjective topic. As we are all different, have different life experiences, and different familial traditions, the reaction to trauma and even the definition of trauma itself will differ. In essence, trauma for you or for me is defined specifically by each of us. This is why we experience two different reactions to the same event.

So, what are some of the effect of trauma? From a physical perspective, trauma can appear as a shaken or disoriented appearance. The individual may appear pale, show signs of fatigue, have poor concentration, shallow breathing, and even heart palpitations. From an emotional perspective, we will see signs of denial, anger, sadness, and even emotional outbursts (sounds like grief and we will get to that). So now, let's compare that to the feelings we have when triggered by shame. We will often experience the very same physical and emotional markers that accompany trauma. Much of this reaction may even be subconscious, and we may have another explanation for it, but ultimately, it is a result of a shame trigger producing traumatic responses.

So, let's look at anxiety for a moment. Anxiety has become a much more discussed phenomena in recent years. People are much more comfortable admitting that they struggle with anxiety. Looking back over the years, I can see where it has played a large part in my life. I knew I struggled with depression even from a younger age, but I had given no thought to anxiety. Many would mistake anxiety for fear. While fear tends to be an emotional response, as well, it is generally associated with real or perceived imminent threat. Anxiety is more about anticipation of something in the future.

For the sake of understanding, I feel like it is important to define terms like depression and anxiety from the perspective of diagnostic definitions. As these are psychological issues, it seems fitting to use the American Psychiatric Association's diagnostic manual of mental disorders (DMS-5) in the discussion. As such, let's define anxiety as an emotion characterized by feelings of tension, worried thoughts, and physical changes such as increased blood pressure. Anxiety can also be caused by specific issues such as separation anxiety in children, fear of heights, enclosed spaces, etc.

Most people may have certain fears that produce anxiety, but there is a kind of anxiety that has as its impetus no discernable reason. This is known as generalized anxiety disorder. It includes excessive anxiety for more days than not over a six-month period and includes some of the physical markers discussed earlier.

Currently, the DSM-5 does not include a designation for anxiety caused by religious belief or causation, although I believe that should change. We are seeing unprecedented numbers of people dealing with anxiety. While many would suggest that the church or some form of religious expression be used to combat such feelings, it is my contention that often religious expression or oppressive belief systems are the true underlying cause. I know several people that have expressed great amounts of anxiety in their younger years as a result of teachings on hell or eternal conscious torment. The idea of burning for all eternity is the stuff of nightmares and late-night horror flicks and yet often, it is central to the Christian belief system. I dare you to tell others that hell is not real and is just a control mechanism for the masses. Go ahead. What you will find is that this teaching is central to "sharing the good news."

In fact, whole ministries have been built around the idea that you must first understand the consequences before understanding just how good the good news actually is. Turn or burn, baby! That sounds like a good reason but isn't that just a manipulation to entice others to acquiesce to your prescribed belief system?

Anxiety can reach levels that are dangerous. That is not to say that generalized anxiety is a walk in the park. The days are becoming less and less that I walk around with my throat tight and unable to swallow, but the reality is there were days when I was positive that I may not be okay. Still, for some, anxiety is more than just a tight throat or a problem being around other people (please hear me, I am not diminishing those things), it is much more problematic. Post-Traumatic Stress Disorder (PTSD) is a result of trauma in an individual and can become a problem for those around the person suffering from it.

We often associate this term with soldiers coming home from war, but we are finding that it is much more prevalent than just that situation. As a matter of fact, the DSM-5 recognizes PTSD in children as young as six years old. That is horrible, yet we are finding more and more cases that involve children because of child abuse situations, but I digress.

So, what is post-traumatic stress syndrome? According the DSM-5, it is "a psychiatric disorder that can occur in people who have experienced or witnessed a traumatic event." To be clear, it can be personally experiencing the traumatic event, witnessing the event, learning about the event as it pertains to family members or friends, or experiencing repeated or extreme exposure to aversive details of the event.

When I was in high school, I did not yet have my driver's license and rode to school with a stepbrother. I begged him one day to let me take the car at lunch to go with my friends. Because we were both young and stupid, he agreed. Unfortunately, it was raining that day. As I returned to school, I approached a traffic light that turned yellow. Not wanting to risk getting caught driving without a license and draw attention to myself for going through the light, I attempted to stop. The roads were wet and slippery, and I slid through the intersection and into a ditch on the other side of the road. Nothing horrible happened, but the car was stuck as there was mud up to the doors, I was covered in mud attempting to get out of the car, and the whole situation required a tow truck to drag the car out of the ditch. I went back to school (covered in mud), and we washed the car on the way home to avoid our parents finding out. For a couple of weeks afterward, whenever I envisioned that accident, my heart would pound, I would sweat, and I cried seemingly without reason. See, not such a bad thing, yet it was traumatic to me to the point of reliving it for quite some time. Now most of the time when we use the term PTSD, it is much more dramatic and difficult. So, why bring this up?

After I was removed from church and was well into questioning all that I believed (or at least what I would allow up to that point), I reached a point where I had to confront my belief on hell. Many have gone through this and seem to have reached some conclusion that brings them peace. I am happy for them, but I have not reached such a conclusion. I still do not know what I believe. I want to believe it is a made-up doctrine based on verses out of translation and context that was used to control the masses, yet there is still this level of fear within me. For a while as I was thinking about this doctrine and trying to come to some conclusion, I would find myself in a panic.

Suddenly I could not breathe, I would sweat, my heart would pound, and once again, I would find myself in tears without cause. I was terrified of hell as a kid (I mean who isn't), and it was often the impetus for better behavior (which just tells you how messed up my theology was anyway). It was the fear of hell, of course, but the bigger fear was being wrong. I mean, if I believe in hell and have some control as far as behavior or begging for forgiveness, then I could mentally deal with the trauma on some level.

My problem, however, were the questions and doubts that kept surfacing. I was terrified of being wrong, coming to the conclusion that hell does not fit God's character, only to find out at the end that I was mistaken. At that point, you have no more options. I thought that I was alone in this fear, but I have had countless conversations in which others shared of their fear on this subject as well.

While I have identified this occurrence as Post-Traumatic Stress Disorder, there is another term that has come into use, Religious Trauma Syndrome (RTS). A simple definition is both the chronic abuses of harmful religion and the impact of severing one's connection with one's faith and faith community. In psychological terms, it is often compared to PTSD and even Complex PTSD (C-PTSD). As I have mentioned elsewhere, not everyone experiencing a deconstruction of their beliefs falls into the category of trauma. Many are satisfied with their new understanding and feel secure in their new view of God. For others, however, there is a daunting experience ahead. This is where I found myself. Religion does a fantastic job of indoctrinating us into a dominant worldview. Our past, present, and future are all explained away in a flurry of prophecy, judgements, and coming atrocities that examined on an emotional level would upset even the most stalwart person.

So, how is it that we function with this understanding, almost acting as though it is preferable? Conditioning. It is amazing at how even the weakest of persons can stand strong in the face of unbelievable violence and disruption and all because they can call it faith. The seduction of an everlasting life makes even the worst situations in the here and now acceptable, almost as a gauntlet of achievement. I have been in conversations in which terrible life events were shared, followed by an "amen and hallelujah" because they were found worthy to suffer for God. The death of a child is because God needed another angel in heaven. The loss of a job and potential financial upheaval is seen as a steppingstone to the next God-ordained mission. We are conditioned to expect the bad and most especially if we step out of the blessing and protection of God.

So now, jump to your own personal experience of stepping away from religion or a toxic theological belief. At first, there is relief and a sense of freedom. The world is yours for the taking and many decide to step out into this new freedom and experience all there is to experience. Some are capable of maintaining this new viewpoint; I was not. I immediately struggled with daunting thoughts of "what if?"

Additionally, those stepping away are often stepping away from many of their relationships as well. Think about how much of your social life is tied up in church activities and friends. For me, it was everything. While I often did not enjoy the crowd and some events made me uncomfortable, I knew I had a place, but we have already discussed relationships.

For now, the overwhelming trauma of betrayal plays out. It is a strong word, but I do not know of another that portrays the emotions I felt at being asked to leave my church. Every friend I had was in that building. My best friend was my pastor and spiritual advisor. I had offered him many glimpses into my past as well as my fears and social issues. To have those summarily dismissed and even manipulated against me was an act of betrayal. I am a loyal person, almost always to a fault, so this kind of betrayal hits hard and stays around for a long time.

I have spent countless hours assessing the entire process of starting to question all the way to being kicked out and agonizing over the role I may have played. I have looked from every perspective to ascertain where I fell short in my role and responses. Over and over, I am able to see a word or an event as something I could have handled better. Yet, overwhelmingly so, it is the betrayal of those that called themselves my friends that has been the hardest to reconcile. There just is no answer except that they were protecting themselves. On good days, I do not hold them accountable because, after all, they were just functioning from their own conditioning.

When one is removed from a community and shunned, they become one of the "others." We all "other" people, but many have made it an art form. Before I was asked to leave, many before me met the same fate. As someone who was close to the pastor, I often heard of these people leaving and the reasons, although I now understand those reasons were only from one perspective. Often afterward and in the course of life, someone who left came up in conversation. Someone had run into them in the community and had learned that they were experiencing a difficult season of life. A divorce, an illness, it does not matter. Always it was surmised that this was a result of them "falling away" and out of God's protection and blessing. It was insinuated that had they just conformed and stayed; this would not be their reality. Remember, conditioned.

Some days, I am afraid that the fear will never go away. I wake up wondering if today will be the day that God has had enough of me and my doubts. Dealing with the subject of death becomes a panic inducing event. I can hardly face any conversation surrounding death because of the overwhelming fear of what follows. On a good day, I will just pass through the hours getting my tasks done and not think about it. On bad days, a cloud follows me and tortures me with thoughts of what is to come. If I still believed in demons, I would suppose that is what is following me. To some extent, it is. It is the demons of an old, conditioned, bullied belief system that does not want to let go. It is religion, and I cannot believe a loving God would condone this type of torture. I just cannot!

PERSONALITY AND TRAUMA

I have mentioned several times those that are able to move on seemingly without issue from a bad religious belief system. I have had conversations with those that cannot understand my need to analyze and consider excessively the pain I feel in the situation. I have lamented on social media platforms that we are all different and handle situations differently, yet it is only recently that I thought about the impact of one's personality on their ability to handle trauma. No one gets off unscathed, but some seem to be affected much more than others. As such, I thought a discussion of personality types and how each type handles trauma and grief was necessary.

I am going to work from an understanding of the Myers-Briggs personality identifier. Most have had some association with this personality testing tool and have at least a limited understanding of where they fall on the spectrum. Let's review for a moment. Myers-Briggs is based on the personality and psychological types as produced by

Carl Jung. There are 16 personality types, and most of us immediately know our letters. I am fond of saying most things exist on a spectrum, and this test just proves it. There is a spectrum for extraversion versus introversion, sensing versus intuition, logic and truth versus feeling, and judgment versus perception. There are differing combinations of each of these, while someone may be technically extroverted, where they fall on the spectrum may be more balanced with introversion than one might think.

It is a fascinating tool on which some curriculums have entire classes. For the sake of disclosure, I am and have always tested as INFJ. So, for those of you keeping score, that means I identify on the introverted side of the spectrum along with being intuitive, feeling, and operate in judgment. That sounds so dire! It depends upon who you talk with but supposedly, INFJs are the rarest personality type. It always amazes me when I read that because I know so many of them.

I do not want to go into great detail here as it pertains to each personality type and trauma but let's examine an overview. Those identifying on the introverted side of the spectrum tend to be more adept at seeking understanding. They often compare and contrast the past and the present and are often stressed by change. They are interested in existential questions and tend toward theories and abstract things. They are often unique (or feel that way) and tend to stay true to their own values. There is a love for logic and a need to know the truth in a situation. They internalize their processes and tend toward a more private consideration of things.

Those on the extroverted side of the spectrum tend to find value in the literal reality of the world. They are extremely detailed and active. They tend to be big picture oriented and finding common ground with others. Harmonious in their interests, they are adept at building rapport, expressing friendly attributes, and being in charge. They work well with others and generally seem to be good at delegating.

Now each of these is a very general understanding of personality. As I mentioned, most of us know where we are on these spectrums and can identify with at least one of these general statements about our personality. So, as it pertains to how each of us handle trauma, we can probably pick out certain things that seem to make sense. As an introvert, I completely identify with needing to understand.

This leads to overanalyzing a situation and ruminating in the results for quite some time. I am overactive in the existential questions and the "what ifs" of life. I absolutely need answers and am often reminded of my inability to be certain about anything pertaining to God. This drives me crazy! Those that are extroverted in this religious deconstruction experience it so differently than I do. As such, I remind myself often and am taking this opportunity to remind you the reader that just because your process was not as difficult (or was more difficult as the case may be), please do not discount the experience of others as less than, obstructed, or just plain wrong. We are just wired differently and have access to different personality tools with which to traverse the journey. Be kind to one another, tender-hearted, forgiving of one another (yes, I do remember Bible verses and try to apply them in my life).

RELIGIOUS ABUSE

Religious abuse has its own diagnosed syndrome as I stated before, Religious Trauma Syndrome (RTS). It is that prevalent. I can hear the screams already from those that disavow such an idea and consider those espousing it as dramatic. Yes, I have been told I am dramatic.

It's hard to imagine, I'm sure. Quite simply, religious abuse includes harassment or humiliation that results in psychological trauma. As with most things, there is a spectrum. I personally know those that were kept from service in their church for having a nose ring as well as many who were sexually abused in the Catholic church. Both fit the description but are obviously different in their effect. Often those suffering on the spectrum of this syndrome are trying to understand their faith and how they personally fit into the narrative.

As with any syndrome, there are symptoms that seem to show up across the board. Let's talk about those a bit. Before I go very far into this though, let me first tell you that it all sounds very clinical, but to those experiencing it, it is far from clinical, it is devastating. As I type, I am fighting tears as just reading and writing about it evokes memories and feelings of failure and disappointment in myself, in others and most importantly, in God.

COGNITIVE

Ah, cognitive function … that which relates to what we know and how we know it. Included in this section is anything that affects how we perceive ideas and situations, our judgment, and our reasoning. Quite often when dealing with abuses that come from religious ideals, three things stand out as problems: authoritarianism, isolation, and fear. Many have had experience with at least one of these and, quite often, all three are involved.

AUTHORITARIANISM

I come from a background full of authoritarianists. First and foremost, I had a very domineering grandmother. Her expectations of me were somewhat out of reach and created in me the need for perfection, which of course is unattainable. It becomes a task master that pushes us to achieve and produce results. Coupled with a domineering person or persons in a life, having an authority figure is compounded in religion by a domineering God. I was told repeatedly as a child that God was always watching and saw everything I did, especially those things that I did wrong.

The god I was brought up with was always seemingly angry and waiting for me to screw up, thereby necessitating some type of punishment. This type of hierarchy is played out in our churches every day. Christianity operates at a level of hierarchy with the masses at the bottom of the ladder while fewer and fewer are in the top echelons. Many have heard of the five-fold ministry.

That of the offices of apostle, prophet, evangelist, pastor and teacher. There are only a few verses within the text of the Bible that discusses these ministry positions, but whole doctrines have been born from the hierarchal model of such ministries. While many are taught that apostles and prophets are the top rungs on the ladder, it is with the expectation of service to the masses. Unfortunately, in my experience, that seldom happens.

Apostles and prophets are to be revered and followed, never questioned. And how does one become an apostle or prophet? Great question! I have received quite a few answers on that one. They all seem to be concerned with the "blessing" of others and them seeing you in that position. (Sidebar: I played a game when I was a kid called "Duck, Duck, Goose." Did anyone else play this game? The premise is that one person skips around a circle places their hand on the heads of the other players and announcing each of them a duck. This continues until they so choose to announce one lucky person as the goose ... not sure why I thought of that. Let's just leave that as it is.)

Authoritarianism as an ideology plays a dark role in religious abuse. It creates environments of control. The lucky one in charge gets to make the decisions even if their decisions do not make sense. In the case of religious abuse, when one is in charge and supposedly hears from an authoritarian god, there is no arguing. How many of you have heard a statement along the lines of "touch not God's anointed"? Sound familiar? Of course, it does because it is used often to control others. We are not to question those in charge. They hear from God, they are higher in the hierarchal society than we ourselves are, and as such, we follow blindly ... or face the consequences.

The authoritarian personality is one of total control. They control the environment, who is allowed into the environment, the actions or responsibilities of those within the environment, pretty much everything. Now to be fair, we can all be pretty authoritarian in our personal realm. I readily admit to being a control freak and wanting everything done my way. Admitting it is the first step ... or so I have been told. So, what is the difference if it is someone in charge of a religious institution? This is where it gets interesting.

Being authoritarian is a psychological personality trait. It is usually accompanied by an ideological attitude. This is where the religious belief comes in. In mainstream Christianity, we have certain tenets of belief that are generally accepted principles. Examples would include: 1) God is holy and just (which extends to a belief that he can, therefore, not abide sin); 2) Jesus is the son of God and the mediator between God and man (thereby insinuating that God is unapproachable); 3) the Bible is the authority on God and the only way in which we can understand him (and in recent years, that the Bible is without error).

I am sure you can think of others as every denomination has their own big-ticket items. Often those that question these main tenets, or the conclusions to which one can come in reference to them, are considered at the very least "back sliders" or heretical. Everything is a spectrum and one person's back slider is another person heretic. Just check my Facebook page on any given day, and you will find that I have achieved the full spectrum, according to many.

Being authoritarian is not just for those in charge. Quite a few would find themselves on an authoritarian spectrum but not necessarily calling the shots. You know the old saying "it takes two to tango"? Well, for a leader to be authoritarian, he must have those who allow him to be so and follow his lead. I grew up hearing that God was a god of order, I mean why else would we be subject to so much information in Leviticus? I mean, really, the lists are endless. So, when you have a room full of people who are authoritarian in their understanding and a leader who leads from that perspective, all seems in order … until you ask a question. Now you risk the ire of the leader who does not like his authority challenged, and you become someone who is deemed dangerous to the rest of the congregation.

I recently had lunch with someone who shared their story with me, and it reads just the way I have explained. A charismatic leader who seems to have a heart for God (and probably does by the way, but just his understanding of God) as well as a large congregation that is intent on sharing the gospel and looks to that leader for direction. The individual that shared the story was good friends with the pastor and was often pointed to from the pulpit as someone to ask questions to when it came to the Bible because she was knowledgeable and studied the Bible a great deal. That is until she studied the Bible and came to a different conclusion on the subject of hell, then her endorsement was removed. She became a pariah to those in the congregation and the eventual outcome was that her friends deemed her a danger and separated themselves from her eventually leading to the pastor and his wife doing the same. Relationships gone and for what, questioning a foregone conclusion in the Christian belief system, the pastor's understanding of it, and the traditional idea of those sitting in the seats. (Sidebar: Can anyone provide scriptural reference for where a belief in hell is including in the "Roman's Road"? Anyone? Bueller? Bueller?).

I have included a few stories communicated to me that I feel fit this area:

"When I was a kid, I attend a church where the children were included in the service for a bit. This time included the music or worship portion of the service as well as a short children's teaching. I vividly remember sitting on the floor one Sunday in front of the pastor who shared a story from the Bible. The story was the one about the bald man and the bear. If I remember it correctly, a prophet was walking by a town and a group of boys from the town began to make fun of him for being bald. The prophet got angry and yelled at the boys then two bears came out of the forest and killed them. The lesson we were to learn was that we should not make fun of others but also, we should listen to those over us in the church so that we did not make God angry. Scared me for weeks!"

JANELLE

"My pastor made the decisions with the help of a board of directors. It was their job to provide feedback and maintain an atmosphere of accountability. As our pastor and the board members at the time had decided we were to no longer be a part of our denomination, it was brought to the congregation for a vote. As it was explained, this was necessary to avoid any interference in how we ran our church or the decisions that were made. The ability of the denomination to remove the pastor at a whim and relocate could leave the church with a pastor that no one knew or wanted in place. Only a few abstained from the vote and the measure was passed. Becoming independent requires an agreement with the IRS as a non-profit organization. Additionally, other elements such as a charter, a mission statement, and bylaws. The bylaws of an organization spell out how the organization will run. Our bylaws created board positions that were to work in conjunction with the pastor to lead the church. Nothing very different from how the church had functioned previously. There were, however, a few added details. First, the wife of the pastor was ordained and installed on the board of directors. Second, all decisions related to the actions of the pastor had to be unanimous in their agreement. If I am not making that clear, if the pastor were to be accused of some violation of the charter or bylaws, it would take every other board member agreeing to act against him. Starting to catch on? There was also a three-member panel that was available to the board members if they had concerns regarding the pastor to facilitate communication and resolve issues. Of course, these three outside members were chosen by the pastor and their contact information was denied to the board members quite a few times. In case I am being unclear ... the system was rigged to avoid the pastor being questioned or held accountable. Now I am sure there are some out there that are wondering how I know these details. Simple, I know because I helped with the incorporation process, read the bylaws, and was privy to the organization that helped set up the new non-profit. Additionally, my husband was a board member until he resigned over these issues.

MICHELLE

"I worked with the children in our church over a period of time. I created lesson plans and taught the children biblical stories. I had created a curriculum surrounding a biblical story for a vacation Bible school and, upon completion, the children were to perform a song and skit in a church service. As they entered the sanctuary, my mother wanting the worship leader to play a certain song, approached the stage to request the song. The daughter of the pastor was on the stage as a part of the worship team and yelled at my mother telling her to get off the stage and sit down. Being somewhat shocked and surprised, my mother did so, removing herself from the room as she was in tears. When the situation was brought to the pastor's attention, a meeting was set up to include my mother, the pastor, his daughter and my father, who had witnessed the situation. My mother is a very quiet and independent person and did not want to make a big deal about the situation. She later also confided that she felt nothing would be done so there was no point in the meeting. As she refused to be a part of the meeting, the pastor called my family and decided that while we were still welcome to attend, my mother was no longer welcome in service until such a time that she could sit and resolve the problem"

MARISSA

Being removed from fellowship due to issues of sin is not unheard of. Many can even make a case for it by using the Bible; let's be honest, I can make a case for most things from the Bible. The term "excommunication" is one which evokes ideas of medieval torture and living in the streets (see, I told you I was dramatic). Seriously, it is the idea of removing someone from fellowship and the sacraments of the church. While historically it referred to the Catholic church, it can be used more generally to explain shunning someone in a religious setting. The word excommunication seems so official, but most that experience a shunning experience do so without any formal ceremony or announcement but rather in the form of quiet removal. A lot of people who experience this phenomenon do not speak out. They are broken, hurt, and often the ideas of their religious ideals spring up and keep them from saying anything. For me personally, when I saw it happen to others, I did not ask why as that would have seemed like gossip, which everyone knows is wrong unless it is in the form of a prayer request.

ISOLATION AND FEAR

The idea of isolation is used quite often in religion. This is very important as almost every person dealing with religious abuse believes themselves to be at fault at least for a time. We assume it must be our issue with understanding. We are confused, and our self-worth suffers. It isn't unusual to find ourselves in the middle of perfectionism and ridiculous expectations for ourselves. I personally have struggled with perfectionism most of my life and found that appearing a certain way in the church environment meant that I was more acceptable. I found myself trying to change who I am. I believed that I needed to be a sweet, soft-spoken, obedient woman who took care of her home and revered her husband. Do not misconstrue me, there is nothing wrong with that if that is who you are.

I found myself continually disappointed in my actions and attitude, constantly striving to be better. Why ... because that isn't who I am. I am brash, opinionated, deeply empathic, and have no problem standing in front of those afflicted. Unfortunately, that does not fit the expectation of a woman in the church, just read the description in Proverbs 31. I have berated myself over and over because I could not fit that mold as have many others I surmise.

These and other ideas are often furthered in a church or religious environment as we are often told "God's ways are higher than our ways" or other religious platitudes that only serve to create an environment of dissonance.

Cognitive dissonance happens when we have inconsistent thoughts or beliefs. So how about some examples? One that springs to mind for me is the idea that God is a god of love but will burn his enemies for eternity, yet we are charged with forgiving our enemies. That can do some major damage to your ideas of right and wrong. We have all at one point or another found ourselves an enemy of God at least in our own minds. Outward appearance secures in each of us the idea that we must hide our "junk" to try to appear the correct way. So, when confronted with people that fall outside our religious ideal (either our own ideal or our church's ideal), we will tend to move away from a relationship with that person. We create perceived us versus them ideals.

We believe ourselves to be part of the "in crowd" while those that fall outside our perceived ideals are considered "lost." Certainly, we should feel sympathy for those that just do not get it, but in the end, they have made a choice and are beneath our concern. I know, I know, I sound very judgmental but that has been my experience and I doubt I am alone. So, while we are expected to believe in mercy and grace, it seems that we end up acting as the God we have imagined. Instead of man being created in the image of God, we have created God in our image, and he suffers for it.

SOCIAL

Often, our religious relationships are the main source of social interaction. Our social structures are built around the relationships that are habitual through the attendance of church. Think of the number of barbeques, potluck dinners, VBS weeks, etc. that you have attended. Often these events are used as an outreach to the community, but almost without fail, it is those within the church that are the main attenders. Those relationship bleed over into pool parties, picnics, and relationships between families. It is all very pleasant and, quite honestly, I enjoyed these relationships for many years. I learned the hard way, however, that these relationships have their limits. The same people that I gave my time, energy, help, and even money will have nothing to do with me anymore. I do not attend their building. I questioned too many things and now seem an enemy. Perhaps I am even now seen as a "back slider" that they shake their heads about and wonder how I could be so lost. Many that end up separating themselves from religion suffer with the loss of these social relationships, it is not just me. It is my personal contention that the loss of these relationships is the most damaging to us emotionally. Every support system we have ever had is gone and we seem incredibly alone.

CULTURAL

Difficulty fitting in and inability to process cultural references or enjoy secular entertainment are all issues for those that are no longer affiliated with their religious institution and belief system. For many, the secular world has been something with which they have had little interaction. As the church community is the main social interaction, there is limited dealings with those in the community. I will say that more and more, we are seeing those within the church struggle with many of the things that are generally associated with the world, or maybe it just seems more prevalent. So much is hidden by those in the church. We believe that we are better than those that use drugs, drink alcohol, or use profanity, yet the church is full of addicts and profaners that act in secret.

EMOTIONAL

Most of us can quite quickly identify here. Emotional symptoms include several of the cycles of grief like depression and anger. Adding to the fun are things like anxiety, loneliness, or lack of meaning in our lives.

So, what causes RTS? Well top of the list for me is toxic theology. This can include atonement theories that cast God as the ultimate cosmic bad guy, hell scenarios, patriarchy ... come on, you list a few as well, there are plenty of examples. So, consider for a moment that you experience this as an adult. You choose to put yourself in a situation that ends up with any of the above experiences. That is bad enough and can affect you psychologically for a long time, but what if that has been your experience since childhood?

For many (actually, I believe most), they are a product of their environment growing up. They are brought up in religious environments that can be damaging, their families support the toxic ideas, and there is an expectation to continue in the environment into adulthood ... and to perpetuate the cycle by introducing your children to the same things. (Sidebar: Does anyone know why railroad tracks are spaced in width the way they are? It has to do with horses pulling wagons and the width of the wagon. Over time, the roads became the path most traveled by those with wagons. There were ruts in the ground and as such, it made sense to continue to use the same path. There was less resistance that way … get it?)

METAMORPHOSIS—PART II

The word "metamorphosis" comes from the Greek and Latin. Ironically, it is associated with the ideas of witchcraft and magic. It is basically a change from one shape or etymology to another. There are as I mentioned previously, different animals and insects that go through some sort of metamorphosis. In reality, humans go through a similar process in utero and even up to and including during birth. But let's go back to the caterpillar because I think there is much to learn about ourselves in this little guy's process. First and foremost, there is no identical process for caterpillars. Each finds their own rhythm and timing, and while I may be guessing here, I don't believe they worry about it. They just live and go along with their eating and existing.

At some point along the way, a hormone that they are used to secreting stops being a part of their experience and throws a new journey at the caterpillar. They have spent a large amount of time eating large amounts of food as preparation for a process that they may not even be aware of. (Sidebar: I know that it was after I started reading large amounts of information and seeking answers from new sources that my process began. It seems like a correlation, but I will leave that up to you to decide.)

Now, it gets interesting ... the caterpillar begins to form a growth inside themselves called a chrysalis which eventually encases the caterpillar and allows for the transformation that is to come. At this point, a decomposition begins, and the caterpillar digests itself and releases certain enzymes that allow for dissolution of its body matter. It sounds pretty gross, but the process is necessary for the metamorphosis. Even while the body is breaking down, the immune system of the caterpillar is continuing to do its job for as long as it can.

Inherent within the structure of the caterpillar, and waiting patiently for their part of the process, imaginal cells survive the decomposition. They alone carry the blueprint for the new creature and begin to appear slowly in the decomposition process. The immune system continues to do its job and attacks the imaginal cells as an unknown, destroying it. Over time, however, the activation of the imaginal cells in comparison to the dying immune system becomes too much. The immune system completely stops functioning and the imaginal cells take over ... the butterfly begins to take shape.

I'm going to stop here and reference a part of the deconstruction process that I have experienced. I want to draw some parallels and hopefully you will see the connection. As I began to question my religious beliefs and several of the long-standing tenets of Christianity, much of what I thought I knew and believed began to cause confusion. This confusion demanded more introspection and inspection and, before I knew it, I was down several different rabbit holes that only provided more questions. I know I am not alone here as I have heard quite a few express the same frustration regarding answers that only leading to more questions in this process. Let me give you an example.

One of the very first tenets of my religious background that came into focus as a matter of questioning was that of eternal conscious torment. In my tradition, it was never referred to as ECT however, it was just called hell. I grew up terrified of hell, and by extension, God. I was convinced that God saw me as an awful sinner, and without going into much detail in this book, there was good reason. I lived my life even as a child constantly begging for forgiveness and hoping against hope that I would somehow make it into heaven, even if God only had to accept me because of Jesus. As I read and studied on the subject as an adult, I found myself continuing to come back to the question of how a loving God could separate those with whom he found fault and sentence them to something that seemed so out of character. After all, I was raised to believe God was love and this seemed far from it.

I know all the arguments and have actually said many of them in conversations with others that questioned the doctrine before I questioned it. God does not send people to hell, they choose it. Hmmm … Why would anyone with all the information choose something so unthinkable instead of God? Further, why would a God who is likened to love create such a place to begin with? Is he unable to reason with people and show them his true character so as to avoid such a conclusion? Anyway, I am not trying to argue for or against hell here but rather set the stage for a comparison to the caterpillar.

As I struggled with this staggering contradiction in my mind and tried to find a reason, I found myself slowing transitioning to the idea that hell is a man-made idea used to control people. I slowly stepped away from the belief and for a short while found a measure of peace. However, along the way I was prone to an almost PTSD reaction that would spring up from seemingly nowhere and that caused panic and symptoms I later learned were akin to anxiety disorder. I would find myself short of breath, with my heart beating out of my chest and an overwhelming feeling of fear. I was afraid of being wrong (again). I would imagine hell and its consequences all over again. Even writing it here, I feel the familiar pangs of panic in my chest and a tightening in my throat.

This sequence played out in cinematic repetition at the beginning of my deconstructive process. I would at strange times need to leave the house and walk and cry and breathe deeply to bring myself back to some semblance of control. After reading about the immune system of the caterpillar as it is dying and the tenacity of the imaginal cells in their ever forward march toward transition, I began to see my situation. The old me is dying, the immune system is still trying to function in the manner it was trained to do. The transformed me, the burgeoning me is struggling toward its own transition and must only outwait the dying immune system in order to gain a sure footing. Suddenly, the process of panic and reasoning made much more sense and, in some small way, became easier to deal with (although I will admit that the panic can still seem overwhelming depending on its time of appearance and the mood in which I find myself).

All of this activity is happening inside the chrysalis. The atmosphere is one of both dying and decomposition as well as birth and new life. It is such a conundrum and yet such a beautiful pattern of growth. The chrysalis itself is a protective environment, yet it came from within the caterpillar as though inherently the creature understood that it must provide for its on transformation and give in to the process in order to grow to its full potential. After more than five years in the process of deconstruction, it has only been recently that I am able to start seeing it as more than just pain and anger. The changes taking place in me are on my timetable and will not look like someone else's process nor will it happen at someone else's pace. I am me; you are you!

I want to interject here and introduce a new transformation to illustrate this point. Most are familiar with another transition that takes place in the animal kingdom, that of the tadpole to frog metamorphosis. My husband and I used to take our children hiking a lot. We live in an area that is rife with multiple hiking venues and intersecting trail systems. It is truly beautiful, and we spent hours on the trails with our children and dogs enjoying the outdoors and seeing all that nature had to show us. One year, after a large amount of rain, we were hiking and came across a large puddle of water that was home to hundreds of small tadpoles. It was an amazing sight to watch them all swimming, and my children were as fascinated as I.

The next weekend we returned to find there were still a lot of tadpoles, but there were also some very small frogs as well as those few that were in between the tadpole/frog stages. It was almost as though they had not yet decided. Once again, we returned a week or so later only to find quite a number of small frogs now hopping about around the puddle while still other tadpoles were at different stages of growth and transformation. It was not long before all of them were gone, however, the puddle was drying up and all the frogs had grown and hopped off to wherever frogs go to live their lives. I have never forgotten that or the sounds of my children's amazement at watching them and coming back to find something new.

I bring this up because in the same video that I watched concerning the metamorphosis of the caterpillar, the subject of the tadpole to frog transformation was addressed as well. Within the conversation with a scientist who studied tadpoles, I learned something new. If you enjoy digging in the mud and splashing through puddles, apparently you can grow up to do the same thing and get paid well for doing so. More importantly, I learned that tadpoles have a say so in their transformation and its timing.

It seems that tadpoles are able to ascertain their environment and evaluate the delicate balance that exists between transforming earlier or later. As with most things, there are pros and cons to both sides. Within the environment of the tadpole there exists some dangers. If, for example, they are in a pond, there is a risk of being eaten while in the tadpole stage, thereby never achieving their metamorphosis. However, if they change too quickly and then transition out of the pond, they find themselves at risk there as well as they are smaller in size. It was actually fascinating to listen as the scientist made the case for both ways. It seems the tadpole has at its disposal some ways in which to influence the process.

If the tadpole feels the watery environment is safe enough to stay longer, they will position themselves deeper in the pond away from the sun and influences that may trigger the transformation. The advantage to doing so is that they gain size while still a tadpole, thus offering themselves a better chance once they do transition into a frog. For those that decide to move to solid ground earlier, they position themselves at a shallow part of the pond and enjoy the sunlight and foods there that will become their main source of nourishment on land.

I bring this up because once again, I find some correlation to the process that we experience and refer to as deconstruction. We are capable of slowing the process or stalling it all together for some time. As I mentioned in my introduction, I hold no on culpable or guilty who says "enough." Those that stall the process or quit asking questions seemingly finding a new safe place from which to live and do so because it is their process. The problem, however, comes when we try to control another's process or decide if their process is authentic. The need to compare seems overwhelming and in my opinion, stems from a place of fear within each of us that needs to know that we are okay. I have friends that were "ahead" of me in this process.

When I was still in church and had barely begun to question the status quo, they were telling me of new understandings of grace, love, and the nature of God. They would jokingly tell me "you just need to truly find God." When my process evolved into a more serious journey and the questions would not stop coming, I chose to go turn inward. I found myself in a self-protective chrysalis (so to speak) that allowed me to deconstruct at my pace. I was careful in my questions and to whom I posed those questions. I felt damaged and broken, confused and angry, but most of all, I felt alone. I did not feel that anyone else understood. I can speak only for myself, but I felt shattered. All those friends that told me that I "just needed to find God" were nowhere because my questions seemed to have surpassed their own. They had found their new normal and were now uncomfortable with my direction and questions. I was climbing out of the pond while they were enjoying the sun and comfort of the warm water.

WHY DO WE DECONSTRUCT?

So, remember the quote from the beginning of the book? An inner impulse or trembling that forces its way out? It sounds so mysterious and to some extent it is, but the reality is that there are multiple psychological processes happening at any given moment that fall outside of our conscious thought. It is in those psychological processes that the answers lie as to why we are ignorant of other beliefs or why we just choose to not acknowledge them. Some of this is pretty amazing and actually makes me feel a lot better as it pertains to all the years that I just did not seem awake.

COGNITIVE DISSONANCE, CONFIRMATION BIAS, AND NAÏVE REALISM

Hindsight is 20/20 or so they say.

Everyone seems to understand that in looking back we can ascertain what "really" happened or make better sense of our understanding of a situation. In the middle of a situation though, I wonder how often people stop and ask themselves what is really happening? I mean the first problem with that of course is how do you know you're in the middle of something? And the view from within the situation is far different than the view outside the situation, that is why it is easier to give advice than to receive it.

Looking back on my religious belief experience, I see the holes in understanding. I see the questions and contradictions. Why did I not see them then? I am sure we can all ask ourselves that question about a lot of different subjects, but in the case of something so closely held as a religious belief, how do we not stop, look around, and ask questions? I remember being baptized. I distinctly remember the feelings of so desperately wanting to be baptized. I begged repeatedly only to be told I was not ready. I remember standing in the middle of the sanctuary with my grandmother and asking once again. The pastor was there as well and asked me what baptism meant. I was only a small child, but I knew. I explained it in my child-like understanding and must have presented a good argument as to my understanding because he decided I was ready.

I remember being scared of going under the water (I had a bad experience in a pool at around 4 or 5 years of age) but knowing this was how I showed God my allegiance. Looking back, that was what I was trying to do. I wanted everyone, but most importantly God, to know I was serious about my desired relationship. I guess I had some magic idea in my head about how I would feel after, yet nothing seemed to change except the expectations of those around me and the expectations I placed on myself.

Growing up in a belief system seems like the right thing. I had wandered away from my beliefs for quite a while in early adulthood only to once again look for God when I had my first child. It is interesting how becoming a parent makes you yearn for some kind of certainty. Once you have a child, you set out to raise them up correctly and if you have a strongly held belief, it is that belief with which you will teach your child. Not many will stand by and allow the child to find their own way, it does not seem like good parenting. I was raised in that way and so were my children. So why is it that we never ask questions even when we see problems?

COGNITIVE DISSONANCE

I believe that cognitive dissonance plays a large part in the discussion of belief systems and our inability to see past them. Most have probably heard of the term but have yet to introspectively evaluate its role in their own lives. The short version explanation is psychological stress felt by a person who is confronted with a belief that contradicts their own ideas or values. Regardless of the evidence presented for the new information, the human psyche defends itself from the clash by seeking a reason for the difference, other than just being wrong.

Leon Festinger was a social psychologist that worked in the field studying cognitive dissonance. It is his contention that human beings strive for internal psychological consistency to function mentally in the real world. In other words, we need things to make sense. So, what happens when we are confronted with information that falls outside our paradigm? Well, we begin to sweat, mentally speaking but maybe physically as well. We need to justify our belief or perspective in order to reduce the dissonance. So, how does one reduce this type of mental disquiet? Well, there are several ways. We can change our minds (come on you know most people who disagree with you religiously are so open to changing their minds, give it a try). Okay, maybe not, but what about changing the rules? Or how about just denying the new information as though it doesn't exist? Ok, I am going to throw some psychological jargon at you. Ready?

"The contradiction of a belief, ideal or system of values, causes cognitive dissonance that can be resolved by changing the challenged belief yet, instead of effecting change, the resultant mental stress restores psychological consonance to the person, by misperception, rejection or refutation of the contradiction, seeking moral support from people who share the contradicted beliefs or acting to persuade other people that the contradiction is unreal"*

Hence a mob if you are familiar with social media. You know how this goes ... you post some new belief or idea that you are contemplating. Rather than discussion or addressing the belief itself, often those responding just simply turn to attacking your character, your background, or just overall ganging up on you to tell you that you are wrong. Rarely will someone engage in actual discussion of the idea itself. You know what I am talking about. We have all had someone tag in their friends or maybe we have done it ourselves. Hmmmm ...

Let's think about this for a moment with an example that happens far too often. Most within Christianity are familiar with end times prophecy. I remember growing up terrified that those around me may just disappear one day and I would be left alone. Strangely, I never seemed to count myself among those that would be raptured ... foreshadowing? Anyway, every little while we are told of a new blood moon, or an impending date arrived at by "serious" study of the Bible and some numerology thrown in for fun. It has literally become a running joke in my social media experience each time one of these doomsday predictions goes by without the end happening. You've seen the jokes, "I survived the blood moon of such and such date!" Those

---

*   Harmon-Jones, Eddie, "A Cognitive Dissonance Theory Perspective on Persuasion", in *The Persuasion Handbook: Developments in Theory and Practice*, James Price Dillard, Michael Pfau, Eds. 2002. Thousand Oaks, California: Sage Publications, p.101.

that truly are sold on "maybe this time" are sincere in their belief, so what do they do when they are wrong? Most will simply explain away the occurrence as incorrect numerology, misunderstood prophecy, or even God simply giving us another chance. How many actually begin to question the belief itself? And if you are one that does begin to question, you are counted among those that fall away and are apostate. Convenient! What is really amazing is that often these missed prophecies actually strengthen the resolve of those espousing the belief. It's like a novice gambling who doubles down after losing.

CONFIRMATION BIAS

So, what fuels this cognitive dissonance? Are you ready for another term? Confirmation bias … we all have it to some extent. This is the human tendency to cherry-pick information that looks and sounds like what we already believe. Ironically to the subject, confirmation bias tends to be most pronounced when it involves ingrained, ideological and emotional beliefs, like politics, religion, or sports teams.

Confirmation bias is like reading the end of a book first and then viewing the book and all its contents from that perspective. Everyone wants to know who did it in a mystery. So, you read the end, find out, and then go back to the book for all the details. In reading the details, you pick up on evidence that points to who you already know to be the culprit. You read through a lens. The same thing happens when we continually expose ourselves to certain news sites and channels. We begin to only hear what we already believe. I am sure by this point you are remembering something learned in church that you are sure is true and you have the articles to prove it. But, are those articles the only perspective? Let's go back to the example above regarding end times prophecy.

I grew up hearing of the rapture and the only argument that occurred was whether it was pre-tribulation, mid-tribulation, or post-tribulation. I read everything I could get my hands on about the subject. Hal Lindsey's "Late Great Planet Earth" was dog eared and worn out from all the times I checked it against what was happening in the world via the news channel. Imagine my surprise when one of the first tenets of my religious beliefs that was challenged was this very subject, and I was told that "Futurism" is only one of four perspectives on end-times prophecy. Not so fast, do you want to know the others? They would be historicist, preterist, and idealist. That's all you get. I am not in charge of your journey, so if you are interested, give them a look. Just beware as all views have their defenders who operate in their own confirmation bias.

So, what is the philosophy behind the phenomena of confirmation bias? It goes back to the early Greeks. In *The History of the Peloponnesian War*, Thucydides is credited for saying "For it is a habit of humanity to entrust to careless hope what they long for, and to use sovereign reason to thrust aside what they do not fancy." Now let's be fair, we have come a long way and maybe our brain is just not wired for all the information it receives. Simple is better and learning or understanding complicated subjects is difficult. How many of us have time to evaluate the importance of quantum physics as we go about our day? Now throw in that quantum physics may hold answers to religious questions and the overall instinct is to push it away and call it silly. Is it? Probably not. There is much to learn in the field of science, yet we generally have neither the time nor inclination to explore it. It makes sense in light of this to look for and defend information that supports what we already believe or have learned. We have taken the verse "do not be conformed to this world" to mean that the world must conform to our ideas.

I do not want you to assume that confirmation bias is only a negative thing. In fact, let's dispense with good or bad, it just exists and how it is used determines its value. Let's consider music for a moment. Music is actually mathematical. The number of beats and rests, the flow of the overall piece, and the anticipation of the next beat is all brain science. Our brains adapt to certain genres of music because we almost know what to expect. There is a satisfaction in anticipating the next down beat and then hearing it just as we anticipated. Our brains are conditioned. Good or bad comes from what we condition it with and how stringent we are regarding how we allow our brains to evaluate new knowledge. So, this brings us to the subject of what I am discussing—religious deconstruction. For those that have started down this path, often you will have no reason as to why the process started. As I have already shared, I can think of no one thing that sparked the internal debate, only that it began and has continued regardless of my comfort levels.

NAÏVE REALISM

This brings me to another similar discussion, one on the subject of naïve realism. Naïve realism is the tendency to believe that how we view the world, politics, or even the Bible, and religion is the objective reality. We fail to recognize that we have a lens or perspective that taints objective reality thereby making it subjective. Everything that we evaluate is an interpretation of the real thing, even God. No one can know for sure who or what God is, we only have ideas. Peter Rollins is an Irish philosopher, and I absolutely love listening to him. He is so intelligent, and he has a great accent. Anyway, I once heard him say that as soon as you begin to describe God, you diminish him. That is a striking thought, one that makes a great amount of sense. Any description we give to God is only able to come from a place of our experience or desire. This becomes problematic in the face of naïve realism. "People's beliefs and perceptions are a function of both the objective properties of the world and the psychological processes that translate those objective features into psychologically experienced features." Even those aware of this phenomenon and take corrective action still are often unaware of just how short they fall in their estimation. We give ourselves a large amount of room in our self-evaluation.

Another expectation within naïve realism is that our beliefs and thoughts are realistic, so it follows that if other people are reasonable, they will come to the same conclusions. It is a projection of our own desires, beliefs, and feelings onto others. Of course, those that share our obvious understanding are considered allies or friends, but those that counter with differing ideas become unreasonable in our minds. Now apply this to political and religious ideas. It is easy to see why we end up so at odds with one another to the point of ad hominin comments, unattractive labels, and downright unchristian like attitudes toward others, all because they refuse to believe like we do.

CONSTRUCTIVE ALTERNATIVISM

I know, I know … I have thrown a lot of psychological jargon at you so far but let's add a little more, so your brain sufficiently hurts. In an effort to reduce uncertainty, science is constantly evaluating ideas for value and objectivity as it pertains to the outcomes. The scientific method of systematic observation, measurement, and experimentation sets the tone for a conclusion. Science and those who work within its realm usually do not have a problem admitting that there is much they do not know, hence the need for continual hypothesis, experimentation, and changing outcomes.

George Kelly was a humanistic psychologist who observed that while the goal of science was to reduce uncertainty, everyday human beings had the same desire. We all like our certainty and it is one of our foundational needs. So, while science creates system and experimentation, human beings create constructs. The goal of both is to postulate something and prove its trustworthiness.

Constructive alternativism is born! For Kelly, the enjoyment of an experience is not the important part, it is whether our outcomes validate our predictions. In other words, people are free to come to their own conclusions based on the constructs they use. As an event can be interpreted in numerous ways, the truth of the event is less important than finding those that seem to interpret in the same way. Allies!

It is not the shared background of a religious understanding as much as it is the construct that is used to evaluate like-mindedness. What do I mean by that? Well, thousands of people claim the same religious construct, but their backgrounds and personalities are not necessarily similar. As such, the construct is their common ground. Out of all the belief systems out there, they have chosen this construct, found their allies, and see the world from this perspective only. Changing this means that the construct itself must be questioned. Now my head hurts!

HERBART'S APPERCEPTIVE MASS

Have you ever had a moment of déjà vu? You know, that feeling that you have done the exact same thing or been in the exact same place before. This happens to me a lot and there are many theories as to why: a glitch in the matrix, neurological disorders, prophetic gifting, and I am sure many others. Somewhere along the way in this journey I began to ponder the opposite. Why had so many of my questions never occurred to me before. I mean some of them seem so obvious to me now, so where was I all that time. I have often compared the experience to being asleep only to wake up where I am currently with all this newfound knowledge. Even better, have you ever been driving only to realize that you arrived somewhere without remembering how you did so? We are so inclined to muscle memory that we just function without a lot of thought sometimes. But this feels different.

For years, I was involved in Bible reading, communion, religious study, and all the activities that make up the religious experience. Yet, nowhere along the way did I stop to evaluate what I was learning or what I believed. I just functioned without a lot of thought. I called it faith; I am sure others would not identify it that way.

I have often stopped along the way now to berate myself for missing such obvious things. I seemingly want to kick myself for never asking why. Not too long ago in the course of my psychological study, I came across an early psychologist and his theory of apperceptive mass. Okay, no glossing over, this is important! Johann Friedrich Herbart was an early philosophical and educational student in the late 1700s to early 1800s. His interests included mathematical application to psychology. As such, and without going into a lot of dusty background, he developed something called psychic mechanics. He believed that ideas had the power to either attract or repel other ideas, depending upon compatibility.

According to Herbart, ideas actually compete with one another to find place within the consciousness. Starting to make sense? As you can imagine, this seemingly puts the mind as a battleground for expression. No idea ever goes away, it just seeks to find its place in the conscious and until such a time, exists in the subconscious. When ideas battle with one another, those that "lose" do not disappear, they just lose some of their intensity and sink into the subconscious. Confused yet?

Think back to your experience of junior high school for a moment. Remember how you were part of a group. For some it was the popular kids, for others the athletes, and for many of us outcasts, but we had each other. Generations have grown up on this idea in movies, and it strikes a chord within us for the underdogs. Okay, now let's apply this same idea to that of our ideas and conscious mind.

Herbart postulated that groups of compatible ideas exist together within the consciousness. He referred to this as an apperceptive mass. Basically, it is all the ideas to which we give our attention. When new ideas occur, they must be compatible with the apperceptive mass in order for us to give it our attention. It is absolutely fascinating. So, let's go back to junior high school for a moment and imagine that all the popular kids are standing together in a group doing what they do. Along comes a new student who looks a certain way, acts a certain way, and is seeking admittance into the group. If that new student is compatible with the group, he or she will be accepted and absorbed. If, however, there is no compatibility, the group will work in concert to repel the interloper.

Herbart expresses this expulsion as repression. The idea does not go away as we have already discussed, but it sinks into obscurity and bides its time. Now imagine that enough of these rejected students end up grouped together. It will not be long before they challenge the power structure for control of the playground. This is where we all cheer and identify with this group in the movies. The underdog gets the girl, the geek wins class president, the new heretical idea gets its day in the sun. Eventually, the repressed ideas will challenge the status quo and force their way into the conscious thought. Voila!

It sounds so simple and yet it obviously is not. This process takes time, maybe even years. I am convinced that this is the answer to my question pertaining to how I could have missed these obvious questions for so long. I did not miss them, they just took time to find their place alongside other new ideas.

THE CORRELATION OF COGNITIVE DISSONANCE AND GRIEF

So, as I have already mentioned, grief is subjective as is the deconstructive process. It is not my place to tell anyone when they have finished grieving or deconstructing. However, one of the issues as it pertains to deconstruction is the idea of rushing the process. That can happen whether grieving a death or intimate life change. Understandably, we want to move past the pain. The problems begin when we force ourselves to move on without examining or experiencing the emotions that are natural to the process. When I first stumbled into this process, I just wanted to feel happy again. In speaking with those who I supposed were ahead of me in the process, I heard things such as "five years ago when this all began" or "I haven't prayed or read my Bible in years," I panicked. How would I survive these feelings for that long? How would I ever be a functioning human being again? Would God wait for me? Was I capable of this and did I even get a choice in the matter? In hindsight, these questions all seem normal now but then all I could do was panic and feel out of control.

Part of the problem is that we still see this process as linear. I question this tenet, then the next, and the next, and so on. That is not how this works. That is not how any of this works! Grieving our ideals and beliefs, and in some cases even God, is not a neat little project upon which we embark with the finish line firmly in our sights. This is a dark, emotional, and in some cases, disastrous event. So, our minds attempt to protect us from the loss and heartbreak by seeking out a reason, and voilà ... cognitive dissonance. We convince ourselves somewhere along the way that we are at the supposed finish line, so when those very real emotions show up again, there is a sense of confusion. We end up blaming the confusion on something else or maybe something we ate the night before.

There was a school of thought within the history of psychology called stoicism. Basically, this ideal is the endurance of pain without expressing emotion. This school of thought taught that the highest good is based on knowledge and that we should be indifferent to pleasure and pain. It is a means of self-control that is often present within those expressing grief. Often, we will put on a happy face, make new relationship connections, and carry on with life. Sitting somewhere in the background are all these unresolved emotions and questions. It would be shortsighted to assume you can move forward with no repercussions. Our emotions always come out, and sometimes in ways in which we wished they did not.

I spoke with an individual who had questioned God and some of the basic tenets of Christianity. They felt sure they had dealt with their emotions and in an effort to return to "normal" found a new church and jumped in with both feet. Every time the emotions would come up and the questions would return, only to be suppressed, convincing themselves that they had already traversed this path and had no reason to return. Interestingly enough, they even wrote a book on their experience in which there was a happy ending, a return to God and church. So, what was the problem?

The absolute breakdown emotionally in the middle of a church service. Out of nowhere, they found themselves reacting to a statement from the pulpit and they could not stop the cascade of emotion and word vomit that ensued. They found themselves on their feet, yelling that none of it is true. God does not exist and if he did, he was a cruel bastard that had no concern for his creation. Dramatic pause ...

So, what happened here? How many of us have felt something along these lines and found ourselves in a conversation in which we were suddenly angry or sad when we thought everything was okay. Of course, most of us do not have this experience, although I will be honest and say that part of the reason that I still will not return to church is because I am afraid of something like this happening. I have an expressive face and roll my eyes a lot when I hear things that I consider bull ... you get the point! We can only convince ourselves that all is okay for so long. In the end, the process wins, it gets its way and we are merely along for the ride. Grief will make its way out whether we choose to recognize it or not.

GRIEF AND ITS STAGES

"Falling Apart

How does one know when they are falling apart? Is there some great sign? Do those around them notice? Or is it that one day you wake up and realize you don't know yourself anymore and that somewhere along the way, you silently and slowly slipped away?

Everyone has bad days. We all struggle with something and sometimes that something takes longer to deal with than other things. But what if what you are dealing with is a long-term ache in your chest, a slow squeezing feeling in your throat that you can no longer ignore? What if all the questions you have had about yourself and all the times you have felt "less than" suddenly without notice decide to fall on you at once? How do you breathe? How do you function? What makes it worth it to even move and do anything?

I have questioned this feeling for quite a while. I have considered hormones, mid-life crisis, boredom, depression, and a host of other emotions and all without answer. What if I am just completely broken? What if there is no coming back from this? For the first time in my life, I am afraid of my own thoughts, not because I don't want to be here anymore, but because for the life of me, I cannot figure out why I should be here.

I have always been told how dramatic I am and right now I feel that way. I am dramatically in pain. I argue with myself all the time to just finish something and that supposes that I am able to even start something. I know there are people in my life that would argue that I bring value and they need me, but is that true or am I just someone they are used to?

I'm not entirely sure when I started feeling this way, but I know without doubt that it increased in September of 2013. I lost family, I lost purpose and definition, and I was basically told that my value was gone. I had been in a place where I was looked to for leadership. I was told all the time that my spiritual talent and contribution was necessary in the body and was important to those around me. I was heralded as someone with a pastor's heart who would be used by God with promises of "having an office just down the hall." I bought it, hook line and sinker! I believed it because I trusted those telling me that. I believed they valued me and loved me. What a joke!"

I wrote the above at some early point in my deconstructive journey. I saved it and not read it again until now as I begin to work on the sections on grief. I will admit ... it hurt to read these words again and feel all the emotion all over again. In all honesty, I am unsure how to begin talking about grief. It is so subjective and emotional that to even try to describe it can only lessen its impact for someone else. So, with respect to all my fellow journeymen, I will only speak about my experience and hope that somewhere within the discussion, there are words of wisdom to others. We are not alone, the emotions we feel are shared by a lot of people, but their application is different as we are different people. I can speak from a clinical perspective about the psychological markers for grief, but it will never encompass all that grief is.

We all feel grief for different things and at different times in our lives. We experience loss, death, and betrayal, and find ways in which to move forward even when it feels as though all is lost and meaningless. Those along the way try to empathize and offer words of love and encouragement, but those efforts often fall short. Many have experienced a loss of relationships as a result of grief. People are uncomfortable in trying to help and often slowly back away. It seems as though most cannot just sit in the darkness with us and allow us to grieve. Adding insult to injury, when a circumstance happens that elicits feelings of grief, we often find ourselves feeling all the grief of every event that has happened in the past. It is a compounding affect that serves little purpose (or so it seems) except to make us question our place in this life. It is heavy, it is debilitating, it is painful!

So, we have covered many of the reasons as to why we believe the way we do for so long. We journeyed into the psychological make up of our consciousness and began discussing this process that so many seem to be experiencing. We have looked at the relationships, the beliefs, and even a little bit of God but now we get to my main point in wanting to discuss this process. Grief!

It is my contention that this process is and/or produces a grief cycle. All the emotions that we feel within this process are in a sense, a grieving process that juxtaposes itself within the cycles of grief that we have all heard about. Grief is not linear. There is no road map or a straight line through the cycles. I have at times felt like I have passed through the anger phase of my journey only to find myself squarely back in that place for a while. All it takes is one trigger and we are off to the races all over again. One more story here ... I am reminded of Romans 12:15, "Rejoice with those who rejoice, weep with those who weep."

Scars are indicative of damage. Some scars are minor, and others are pronounced and will never go away. As I write this, I am sporting some really interesting bruises that upon close observation could be construed as abusive. Are they? No, they are not. They are a result of an activity that I chose to participate in and worked hard to accomplish. The bruises are ugly and quite honestly, they hurt, but I am aware that they will fade pretty quickly. Currently however, I am keenly aware of them and remember with clarity the activities that produced them. So, we could say they serve as a reminder of an event or multiple obstacles in this case. Once they fade, I will remember the event, but the pain associated with the events will fade into obscurity. This same response is why many women have more than one child, they forget the pain (right, ladies?).

What happens however when the scarring is much more severe? Several years ago, my youngest son was injured in a pool accident. His skull was fractured, and he was taken to the hospital where he remained for several days. One of those days was spent in the intensive care unit as he had lost sensation on one side of his body. The good news is that he recovered and has full use of his body. He does, however, have a significant scar on the back of his head where he struck the pool, requiring stitches to close the wound. The scar is pronounced and visible because his hair is cut short. If he grows his hair longer, the scar will be covered but it will still be there.

So, what makes this scar different? The sensitivity! For some reason even touching the scar is incredibly painful to him. That may fade further but it is still an issue currently. Not too long ago, his brother hit him with a marshmallow (yes, a marshmallow … we throw them in my house, don't judge!). The reaction was immediate pain. He put his hands protectively over the scar and yelled in response.

So, what is my point? I was recently confronted by someone from my church past who decided that I needed to stop playing the victim and just get over my pain. I had not heard from this person in five years, not since the day I walked out of the building for the last time. I thought we were friends. I held him no ill will, yet we are no longer in touch … until that moment. His comment brought back all the pain and emotion. I felt the rejection all over again. My heart constricted and the events that led to that occurrence seemed suddenly altogether too much again. I have a scar, one that will apparently last quite a while.

Don't get me wrong, I don't sit around daily revisiting those emotions and events. Most of the time they don't even come to mind anymore, but every now and then a marshmallow hits me. I am once again confronted with something that caused significant pain in my life, and I react defensively trying to protect myself and my emotions all over again. I hope that fades as well. Right after this event, in the course of conversation with my husband, I uttered the words "time heals all wounds," to which my husband reminded me of the marshmallow and the scar. Apparently, healing is different for all of us, just like grief and deconstruction.

As we come across those people who are grieving either a death, a marriage, close relationships, or even grieving their traditional understandings of God, let's keep in mind that our experiences in no way have a bearing on the length and severity of their experience. We cannot project onto them our way of handling things. Instead we should rejoice with them when they rejoice and mourn with them while the mourn. Love holds one another up, it does not throw marshmallows or bricks (whatever the case may be).

There is no right or wrong way in which to grieve. It is this very idea that hurts so many when they are going through a sorrowful time. People may want them to just move on or express the pain in a more positive way. Just writing that pisses me off, because no one should tell me or any of you how to deal with our grief—not its content, not is expression, and not its length of time.

There is a sense of helplessness in the process of deconstruction that shows up in the grieving process. We seem to be a victim of the circumstances and the emotions that line the road of this journey. Just as deconstruction is often imposed upon us, so too grief with its pitfalls seems to just show up in the circumstances. So how do we handle it all? I am sorry to say that I do not have all the answers, just experience. Maybe that is the best thing. Experience allows us to empathize with those we encounter along the way. It enables us to sit quietly and mourn with those that mourn. We understand the pitfalls and missteps that are going to be a part of all of this. We can listen, nod our heads, and cry alongside others.

DENIAL

Most assume that this stage of grief means that you deny the traumatic event took place at all. For some that may be true, but often those in denial are looking for loopholes in the story. Denial allows for a period of being numb, protecting the individual from the hurt that will eventually follow. Think for a moment of someone who has received a bad medical report. Often there is a hope that medical lab results are confused, or the doctor did not read the results correctly.

Anything that will change the outcome. You may think this is mentally unhealthy but quite honestly, this is your subconscious protecting you for a bit. This is the duality of actual reality to preferred reality.

So, as it pertains to the subject of deconstruction in my experience, I was aware of all the questions and seeming inaccuracies about God, but I just kept holding onto what I knew and claiming faith. I demanded that the devil stop tempting me with these obviously false accusations and questions. I imagined that I was somehow a mighty warrior for God and as such, was facing the anger of the enemy. I wanted so badly to believe anything that would allow me to continue in my ignorance rather than facing the questions and the answers that might just be more than I could handle.

In this stage, we avoid the questions and confusion. When fear begins to overtake us, we hold firm to that which we have always known. There is a sense of elation at being found worthy to be tested for God ... . anyone? This feeling eventually fades, and while this begins a time of painful realization, it is where the healing actually begins. I know it is an unpalatable example, but I am reminded of a burn victim.

Those who experience severe burns often will not feel pain for a while. The nerve endings are destroyed, and there is a need to imagine the damage is not as bad as we fear. Eventually, however, in order to heal, debridement must occur. For those unfamiliar with the process, the dead burned skin must be removed. Yes, it is as bad as you image. It is a literal tearing away of the dead and damaged skin in order the healing process to be successful. While I have repeatedly said that the grief process is not linear, I do believe that for many anger follows this denial stage because the process of removing the dead and damaged beliefs will piss you off pretty quickly once the reality of the situation finds you.

ANGER

I personally struggle with a bad temper. It usually comes about fairly quickly, burns brightly, and then fades. For others, the anger percolates at a low level of heat, occasionally flaring up, but just simmering under the notice of others for quite some time. I prefer my method of "losing it" as I find it passes much quicker, but I do recognize that it can be traumatic for those who are my target … just ask my husband! As I have mentioned previously, some experiencing deconstruction have arrived here under circumstances that are not traumatic. As such, there experience with anger may be short-lived if even noticeable. There may be momentary flashes of frustration or irritation, but it is quickly dissolved. For others, however, this stage may last for quite some time. As I am sure you have picked up on, I lived here for quite some time. I often find myself back in a place of anger based on circumstances that come up or problems that others encounter for which little answers exist or instances in which they have been treated poorly.

It is here that we will often hear "Where is God?" or "Doesn't God care?" Please know this is normal. This does not mean you are broken. This does not mean you have failed. Please stop and hear me! You are okay. If you need to scream for a bit, please do! It is helpful to think of this stage as a strength. It grounds you in the reality of the situation and allows you to feel the weight of the issue, its importance to you, and your ability to deal with it. I have to tell you, I heard *be angry but do not sin*. I could not pull that off. I was angry a lot, for a long time, and probably said and did many things I would not normally. I often feel some regret over that, but most of the time, I embrace it. It kept me searching. It kept me moving forward and not settling once again for whatever someone else told me I should feel.

Of course, there are levels of anger that are unhealthy and that is why it is good to have people around you in this process to serve as a sounding board. I'm available to anyone that needs to yell and vent. Find a safe space and let loose, its cathartic!

BARGAINING

"I'd almost consider going to church again, anything to distract me from what's going on inside of me. 'Freedom' is too difficult a burden to bear for most people. Indeed, I am one who finds its weight exceedingly heavy at times.

I look back and wish sometimes that I didn't set off on this journey of self-discovery, and yet, I sense deep down that I was compelled to do so by some hidden force. Let's say, for argument's sake, that this hidden force is God. I'd like to think it is, but I have no way of really 'knowing.' Oh yes, my faith albeit a little tattered is intact and I ask often, 'Who are you, God, and who am I?'

The rabbit hole is deeper than I ever imagined, full of peril and danger, and is not a very pleasant place to be.

It's scary down here.

Still, as the vagabond that I am, the hero, I must continue on in spite of my fear of the unknown, wield my sword in trembling hand, and fight the ghouls and monsters who so ardently desire to keep me from knowing that freedom, the heaviest matter in the universe, is attainable, within."

Bargaining is a normal part of a grief cycle. The event leading to grief often leaves a large hole in the emotional body of a person. As such, the desire to find equilibrium and normalcy is strong. We have all seen movies or television shows in which a character faces a loss or the danger of a loss and pleads with God for a favorable outcome. Even the Bible provides a story in which a king begs God to save a child. We decide what we are willing to give up in order to return to a favorable position. If I just try hard enough, if I go to church every week and read my Bible, maybe I can appease God and ask for my heart's desire. The temptation to see God as a Deus ex Machina is overwhelming. For those of you unfamiliar with the term, think bubble gum machine and you have the quarter. Does God work that way? Many believe he does work that way.

In the midst of a deconstructive experience, when one or many beliefs are on the table for examination, the sudden realization that all is not what we thought can be an earth-shaking event. Let me give you an example. When I began to question eternal conscious torment, you know, the belief that God will abandon those with whom he has no relationship to an eternity of fire and brimstone, it was a big shift. Do not get me wrong, the idea that no fiery furnace awaits you in eternity is a welcome shift when one has lived their whole life terrified of just such a place, but this will eventually lead to a question about heaven. Is it what I think it is or am I once again, wrong? Going down this road will lead you to a place of panic, pain, and bargaining to just go back to what you once knew.

DEPRESSION

"Today I heard the cave call me ...

I'm sure most have no idea to what I am referring but I heard it. I have bad days like everyone else. I have days where I just want to be left alone, but for the most part, those days are few and far between, now. That hasn't always been the case. I spent years of my life struggling with depression. I hid it from most people because it is not a pretty subject and many will just disregard it anyway. It makes people uncomfortable. I mean, let's be honest, it makes me uncomfortable, yet there it is.

I liken it to a cave because it has a sense of darkness about it. It is supposed to be hidden or at least that is what we are told. I've always hated the cave yet often that is where I felt the most comfortable. The voices and words were familiar and most often, they were my own. The running diatribe of feelings that we have about ourselves that just seem to go on. As I said, I fought them for years, yet strangely, they had another source. In the course of my religious upbringing, faith was a big subject. We just have to have faith. We hear it all the time, if you are sick, just believe that you are healed. Are you in debt, just believe for it to be miraculously paid, it's faith, brother! But what happens when you are aren't healed or the debt doesn't go away? Well, the obvious answer is that you didn't have the faith. I mean, after all, just get over it. It is self-ish to feel the way you do ... the cave is calling ...

Those voices seem to be louder now on the outside of my cave. Those voices come from those that are supposed to know mercy and love. Those voices come from those that call themselves leaders and then chastise me for being broken. The funny thing is, I don't feel broken. I feel sad sometimes and I want to be alone sometimes, but I am not broken. The cave starts to look better and better because at least there, the only voice is mine, or is it? I heard the cave call today ... .

I'm sure this sounds very scary and sad, and yet I don't see it that way. I am a loner. I always have been uncomfortable around others. I have great empathy for others, and I have no issues helping others and wanting to make a difference yet at the end of the day, I want to be alone. I don't attend church anymore for a lot of reasons and today someone said that was selfish. That hurts! Why are we all so sure we have the right answers, for ourselves but most pointedly, for others? The cave is calling … .

What is so special about the cave? I have presented it as pretty negative up until now, but it isn't. I think it is the realization that I'm not alone. Jesus sits with me. He sits quietly and just maintains an even presence. He doesn't tell me I need to get over it. He weeps with me. He doesn't tell me I am selfish; he lets me know that I am valuable just as I am. He smiles with me; he laughs with me. He doesn't chastise me for not having enough faith, he has it for me. I heard someone say today that the opposite of faith is not doubt but certainty. That is who Jesus is to me … my faith. I don't have to be certain, he is, about me and everything. Yeah, the cave is calling … "

I wrote this a while back as I contemplated the deep sadness and downright depression that often accompanies a shift in your belief system. There is a pulling in, a hiding of the emotions to protect oneself in the face of those who misunderstand or get angry. Depression is insidious. It takes up room in our minds and fools us into thinking we are the only one suffering. It begins to mold the individual into a recluse who, when faced with the daunting prospect of being around others, puts on an act and pretend that all is well when, in reality, they are dying inside.

Depression can result from a lot of things. Some feelings of sadness are short-term and are brought on by events in our lives that demand sadness. It hurts, and I am not dismissing it at all. We have all felt it at one time or another. In addition to this type of depression, there is a type that is longer in its endurance and more demanding on our physical bodies. The mind becomes cluttered with an overwhelming sadness that seems to have no rhyme or reason, or at least one that explains the crushing weight that seems to sit on your chest most of the time. The toll on the physical body is one that can include sleeplessness, anxiety, inability to eat among others. In my experience, I would get up every day and wander through my responsibilities unsure of how I would finish the next one.

Questioning your beliefs demands a lot of you mentally. When you think you have a deep understanding of a process or a belief only to find out that you were wrong, the natural response is to question everything, maybe not right away but you will get there. Eventually, you will question even your own thoughts and existence. The big question of why I am here will suddenly loom in front of you and all the assurance that you used to experience about purpose and meaning will pale in the light of this big question.

When I began to question my beliefs about God, one of the first was that of the angry God. It has always seemed as though God were this angry deity that was only appeased because of Jesus. I spent a good amount of my younger years imagining that the only reason God accepted me was because I had said some magic words and accepted Christ. God, by extension, was then bound to a contract which included accepting me. I believed it to be begrudgingly, and if God had his preference, I would not have made the cut. I am sure you can see the self-image issues there.

I started asking questions about grace and mercy. I wanted to understand how others viewed God. I had always assumed that it was close to how I viewed God. Imagine my surprise to find that others had a completely different experience and had a loving father in heaven. That in and of itself is certainly not a reason to deal with depression; however, the poor self-image still rules the day and I ended up feeling that I was unworthy of that kind of acceptance. The more I thought about who I actually was, not the person that I allowed others to see but the real me, the more I realized I was not worthy of a God that would just accept me.

ACCEPTANCE

"Sometimes we must completely let everything we once believed go. There were about 3 years where I was agnostic on my good days and hard-core atheist on my worst. I found that for me, I had to completely stop believing in God for a while, to detox of toxic theology, so to speak, before I was ever able to even attempt to pick it back up. It's been a slow process of picking things back up. I slowly moved back in taking pieces, trying them on for a while, discarding, trying on again once I had more information, etc... For me, that's what faith is. The problem with religion in the world today is our demand for certitude. We're not ok with not knowing. So, we develop systematic theologies to answer every question. It doesn't matter if the answers we create are good or Holy if they are certain, and then we cling to them like a life raft afraid of being swallowed by the river beneath us. Once I let go and simply fell into the river of God, I found that it's currents take me where I need to go, and rather than being terrifying, they're life giving. Sometimes I still cling to things when the current gets too fast or I hit too many obstacles. But I try to remind myself that the water is fine."

In all honesty, I am not sure how to write about acceptance. I have no idea what it looks like for me. I see glimpses of it in other people and wisdom in some of their suggestions, but the concept eludes me. The general overall idea of acceptance is one of coming to an understanding of what has transpired and finding peace within. The problem with this idea as it pertains to deconstruction is that the questions generally do not stop. There is always more to learn. So, in trying to reach a place of acceptance, one must become acquainted and comfortable with questions and the tension between certainty and uncertainty.

Another common idea of acceptance is that of returning to a place of "normal." The most obvious response to that is who decides what is normal, but I digress. If we were discussing grief associated with a death, we would understand that normal will never look the same again. There is a hole where that person used to be. Our emotions surrounding that person and the situation that removed them from our lives will not allow us to return to the old normal. We must look for the new normal. Deconstruction is no different, you can never go back to what you once knew in the same way. Even if during the process you come back to an idea that you had thrown out, you will still see it differently. So, what is the answer?

METAMORPHOSIS—PART III

Okay, let me get back to the caterpillar. He has had some time in the chrysalis and has gone through major changes in form and function. The imaginal cells (I'm sorry but how amazing is the name for these cells?) have done their job and a new creature waits to burst into the world. If you have ever studied or read about frequency, we can legitimately say the caterpillar now vibrates to a new frequency and as such is defined in an entirely different manner. It is almost the moment we have all been waiting for, the butterfly is formed, the metamorphosis is complete, all that remains is the big reveal. The chrysalis has become transparent and now showcases the new creature. I love this idea of transparency especially after the time of being hidden away. Once again, I find a beautiful correlation. Where much of our deconstruction is done within ourselves and is hidden away from others that might interrupt the process, there comes a time when we begin to become transparent. Just as the chrysalis slowly becomes transparent, so do we, slowly allowing others to hear our questions and see our process. We venture out carefully in order to still protect ourselves as well as develop new muscles in our reasoning. Until the day, we are sure we are okay.

THE GOOD SHEPHERD AND GOOD FATHERS

One of the most daunting of feelings in all of this is that of being alone or on the outside. We no longer feel a part of the group and have been rejected to the point of wondering if we belong anywhere. Many like myself, no longer attend a building, and we struggle to find those relationships that will honor our process and accept us even if we no longer accept God or religion. In all honesty, I have struggled with God for almost seven years now. It is not the struggle of my youth and early adulthood in which I was just trying to be good enough, rather it is now a struggle to find God good enough.

I struggle to reconcile the view of the God presented to me and the God that I feel should exist. I want to believe and find peace and comfort in that relationship once again, but I need to know that God is worthy of my effort and not just some tyrant. I want the loving God, the merciful God, the gracious God. I can already hear the push back … *So you want your version of God, but not the true God?* Nothing could be further from the truth. I do not want a God that I can describe or imagine. He should be better than I can come up with. I read a statement from Peter Rollins at some point. While I do not remember the exact wording, it was along the lines of every time we try to describe God, we diminish him. God forbid that my image of God be the totality of his character.

Now saying that, let me further state that I would hope that God would at least look like all the positive attributes that have been assigned to him. Those should be included. I have spent so many years hearing of all the people that God will not accept that it is easy to find myself among them. I mean who does God accept since we are all a mess? Glad you asked! I found myself picking up my Bible again this morning to answer that question. (Sidebar: I waited for the lightning strike, but so far, so good!) I found myself reading some parables and several stand out to me. The first being the parable of the lost sheep. I know we have all heard versions and interpretations of this parable, but I wanted to go back to it for research purposes.

> "What do you think? If a shepherd has a hundred sheep, and one of them has gone astray, does he not leave the ninety-nine on the mountains and go in search of the one that went astray? And if he finds it, truly I tell you, he rejoices over it more than over the ninety-nine that never went astray. So it is not the will of your Father in heaven that one of these little ones should be lost."
>
> MATTHEW 18:12-14

I have always enjoyed this parable. It reminds me that God seeks after those that are lost. I think most of us see ourselves as that one, and Jesus is suggesting that he has left the 99 for us. We are that important! Let's look at the parable in context to the surrounding text. Jesus and his disciples are in Capernaum, and much discussion is going on between the disciples. Jesus has just explained that he is going to be betrayed and killed. So of course, the disciples bring the conversation back to themselves. Who is the greatest? Who sits where? The obviously important questions. Even John (the disciple who Jesus loves; and we know this because John tells us) brings up those doing miracles in Jesus' name, and his desire to smite them for it because they are not one of the cool kids (disciples, in case you missed my sarcasm). In response, Jesus tells this parable. His obvious assertion is that they will agree that the good shepherd goes after the one even at the expense of the 99. What is the shepherd's response at finding the one? He rejoices! In Luke's version, he even puts the sheep on his shoulders and carries it home, calling all his friends together to rejoice with him. It is the last verse in the parable however that makes the point. It is not God's will that any should be lost. My question to you in this is does God get his way? I believe he does. So, when I find myself on the outside looking in, trying to find my place, and deciding if God is good, my question will be answered. If God is truly there and a good God as we have all heard, there is no question too difficult, there is no doubt too large, there is no process through the darkness that can keep God from us. Notice I did not say "us from God"? It has never been about us seeking God but always been the other way around. On good days, I remember this. On bad days, not so much. While I have a lot of bad days, my choice is to believe that God is still seeking me, and if I am considered lost, it is because I belonged.

The second parable is another that most are familiar with, the prodigal son. I have always thought this parable is misnamed. While the prodigal son plays a prominent role in the story, the father is the main character. Most know the story, the younger son leaves home with his inheritance and squanders it before finding himself alone, broken, and near death. He decides to return home and beg his father for the lowest place in his household. The scene Jesus paints is that of a downtrodden, broken boy slowly making his way home only to be confronted by his father racing toward him with joy. The obvious message is one of forgiveness on the part of the father, yet it is bigger than that. Nowhere do we see the forgiveness happen after a confession of guilt, rather the joy of the father is evident while the boy is still a long way off. Forgiveness was given long before it was asked for. There is so much reassurance in that message. No matter how far I have roamed, no matter how much I have messed up, no matter how long I have wandered and questioned, God waits, and forgiveness has already been given. I do not think it was ever a question of being withheld.

Now I will admit that a part of me is still sitting here thinking, *Great, but that in no way helps me through this process*. Yet, as I think about it, it actually does. I am free to take as long on this journey as I need. I am free to evaluate all of God and my interactions with him. I am free to struggle, to process, to wrestle, to avoid, to be angry, to be sad, to debate, or to reject, but it is never too long for God.

WHAT IS NORMAL?

You are going to hate me I'm sure, but the answer is I do not know! So, you have come all the way through this process, hoping for a conclusion only to find that the story continues. It continues because it is your story, your process, your grief, your deconstruction! You get to decide. For myself, on my good days, I find peace in the normalcy of my schedule and can put it all out of my mind and enjoy my life. On my bad days, I struggle and argue with myself and God (along with many of you if you are on Facebook). At the end of the day, I must admit, however, that I still do not know and be okay with that because it is my new normal.

So how do we go about living in the new normal? It will be different for each of us, but, overall, it is a decision to investigate everything until we are sure it is of no use. Richard Rohr has a book called *Everything Belongs*. It is a book on contemplative prayer and according to his description, it is a book for those seeking a deeper spiritual life. Contemplation is nothing more than thought. About what? Whatever we choose. In this case, the subjects of God and theology are the focus but, in all reality, we contemplate in order to understand. Is there a guarantee of understanding from merely considering and questioning? Unfortunately, no! But we can find peace in the process.

We are focusing, asking, seeking, and if we are lucky, finding answers along the way.

Allow yourself the journey! Do the work! Ask the questions! Be kind to yourself along the way as well as to others! Be okay with being wrong, we all are!

METAMORPHOSIS—PART IV

This is where I like to think and imagine the process along the lines of a poem or a fairy tale. I imagine not a pecking away at the chrysalis like a baby bird chips away at a shell, but rather that the emerging creature takes a large new fulfilling breath and the expansion of the self can no longer be contained within the protective shell. It is time to emerge. I envision the brand-new creature crawling slowly from its enclosure only to turn and reverently hold the chrysalis of its metamorphosis like a new mother cradles the face of a newborn baby. If it were to communicate its thoughts to the chrysalis, they would be something close to reverence and awe at its ability to hold space for the new creation, allowing a safe and perfect transformation. Finally, I imagine the interaction to include thankfulness for the process, even the pain and feelings of dying, because it took all of these parts of the process to produce the new creature that will lift its wings and fly where it has never been before.

REFERENCES

1. American Psychiatric Association. (2013) *Diagnostic and statistical manual of mental disorders: Diagnostic and statistical manual of mental disorders* (5th ed.) Arlington: American Psychiatric Association.

2. Bell, R. (2012). *Velvet Elvis: Repainting the Christian faith.* New York: Harper One Publishing.

3. Brown, B. (2007). *I thought it was just me: Women reclaiming power and courage in a culture of shame.* New York: Penguin Group.

4. Caputo, J. D. (2007). *What would Jesus deconstruct? The good news of postmodernism for the church.* Ada: Baker Academic.

5. Distefano, M. J. (2018). *Heretic! An LGBTQ-affirming, divine violence-denying, Christian Universalist's responses to some of evangelical Christianity's most pressing concerns.* Orange: Quoir.

6. Festinger, L. (1957). *A theory of cognitive dissonance.* California: Stanford University Press.

7. Hagberg, J. O. (2003). *Real power: Stages of personal power in organizations* (3rd ed.). Salem: Sheffield Publishing Company.

8. Jacobson, R. (2016). *Unchurching: Christianity without churchianity.* Unchurching books.

9. Kafka, F., & Corngold, S. (1981). The metamorphosis. Toronto: Bantam Books.

10. Manning, B. (2000) *The Ragamuffin Gospel.* Colorado Springs: Multnomah Publishers, Inc.

11. Packard, J. and Hope, A. (2015) *Church refugees: Sociologists reveal why people are done with church but not their faith.* Group Publishing.

12. Rios, K., DeMarree, K. G., & Statzer, J. (2014). Attitude Certainty and Conflict Style: Divergent Effects of Correctness and Clarity. *Personality and Social Psychology Bulletin, 40*(7), 819–830.

13. Rohr, R. (2003). *Everything belongs: The gift of contemplative prayer (2nd ed.).* New York: The Crossroad Publishing Company.

BOOK ISH:
THE CANNON CONTINUES

The podcast that's dismantling the sacred/secular divide book by book, with your host, Michelle Collins.

www.bookish.cc

Many voices. One message.

Quoir is a boutique publisher
with a singular message: *Christ is all.*
Venture beyond your boundaries to discover Christ
in ways you never thought possible.

For more information, please visit
www.quoir.com